RUN BETTER, RUN FASTER

USING A BIOMECHANICAL APPROACH

Herb Kieklak
USATF

Culicidae
PRESS, LLC
culicidaepress.com

Ames | Gainesville | Lemgo | Rome

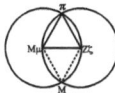

Culicidae Press, LLC
918 5th Street
Ames, IA 50010
www.culicidaepress.com

editor@culicidaepress.com

Culicidae
PRESS, LLC
culicidaepress.com

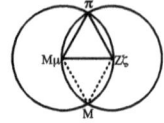

Ames | Gainesville | Lemgo | Rome

If you have any health concerns, please visit your doctor prior to
beginning any physical fitness program.

Cover design/image and interior layout © 2015 by polytekton.com

Acknowledgements

Coach K would like to give a special thanks to all of his students and clients who patiently acted as 'test subjects' while we developed the biomechanical approach

CONTENTS

CREDENTIALS AND CONTACT INFORMATION

N.S.C.A. – Certified Strength and Conditioning Specialist
N.C.S.F. – Certified Personal Trainer
U.S.A.W. – Certified Sports Performance Coach
U.S.A.T.F. – Certified Track and Field Coach
A.A.S.D.N. – Certified Nutritionist
Certified – Strain/Counter Strain muscle release technique
Certified – P.N.F. level 1 Core and Extremities

Email: herb@coachKfitness.net
Web: www.coachKfitness.net

FOREWORD

The idea for Grab'N'Go running came to me one morning during a training session. I was wondering about the possible correlation between older recreational runners—who always finished at the top of their age groups—and the fact that they had run back in high school or college. The options were:

1. **Genetics:** possibly, but many recreational runners would also have the same good genetics, yet not run as well…back to square one.

2. **Prior Experience:** probably true and important but that can be matched by late-starting recreational runners…back to square one.

3. **Fitness Level:** not likely, since many of them had quit for years due to family or work, etc. and then got back into running… back to square one.

Then came my eureka moment. I realized that they had probably started their run training with spikes! This is very important: most people think about the obvious benefit of traction. Yes, that is true and it offers a big benefit. But more importantly, spikes provide a traction or grabbing sensation which then allows the famous Posterior Kinetic Chain (PKC) musculature to activate and work much more efficiently. However, these runners were now running *without* spikes and still doing well, so there must be another reason. Eureka again: the time that they had spent running with spikes had created a neuromuscular pattern or muscle memory that was still working. This pattern is much more efficient than what conventional runners use. Conventional runners who learned without spikes just ran on the ground with a hit-and-push-off style.

From that moment on I began to work on how to develop the same sense of traction into my training so that the PKC musculature would activate at foot strike. After that idea kicked in I began to add in the rest of the system that makes up the Grab'N'Go program.

INTRODUCTION

This book is written to help both current runners—and those who want to become a runner—learn how to run more smoothly, more efficiently, and for longer periods of time without injury. We wanted to get rid of the painful early sessions that go with learning to run the traditional way (I used to hate running when I first started). We feel there is no need to "pound the pavement" or feel all beat up after a run (muscle soreness and hard work are OK, feeling beat up is not).

Here is what we are going to cover in this book:

1. Screening for Potential Injuries Before You Start
2. Biomechanics: learning good technique always beats "getting stronger". This is the main argument of the book.

3. The Key Points that make up the Grab'N'Go system:
   — Five parts of running.
   — Symmetry of arms and legs.
   — Posture for ergonomics.
   Master these areas before putting more time into anything else. It may take a bit longer to learn but pays off in the long run (this is important!).
   We include the appropriate strength and coordination drills for each section, as you need a certain level of strength in order to perform each technique correctly.
4. Build the Machine
5. Speed or Distance? This seems to be the big conundrum for runners. I know I used to think that it was an either/or choice. You were either a distance runner or "one of the speed guys". I now realize that this is no longer true. With a little planning it is possible to work on both parameters as they each have their own benefits. Below we discuss how these very different goals can be merged.
6. Common Injuries and Simple Remedies: none of us like going to the doctor. However, every runner at some point or another will experience these, just like falling down and scraping your knee when you learned to ride a bike.

Chapter 1:
Screening for Basic Structural Components

After years of coaching runners of all levels, this has now become my first step. I used to meet runners at the track and immediately start working on 'track drills' and then would become frustrated as many beginning runners could not perform these new techniques without problems. The old-school approach of "just keep working harder" only produces more of the same results. I start with the Client in what I call 'Runner Position' which looks a runner in mid-stride position.

WHY? If the athlete/runner exhibits any of the following faults in simple static standing, imagine what is happening to their hips and knees when they run and they increase the impact on landing to two to three times their body weight.

In this position, I look for several key points:
- Is their Center of Gravity (CoG) over their base of support/stance leg? This is best tested from a side view (Fig. 1a and 1b).

Fig. 1a: Correct stance: CoG over athlete's base of support.

Fig. 1b: Incorrect stance: CoG shifted forward
of athlete's base of support.

- Do they have equal weight distribution on their foot? Or is it skewed to the toes/ball of foot which will increase knee pressure and therefore pain. Again, a side view works best (Fig. 2a and 2b).

Fig. 2a: Equal weight distribution on foot.

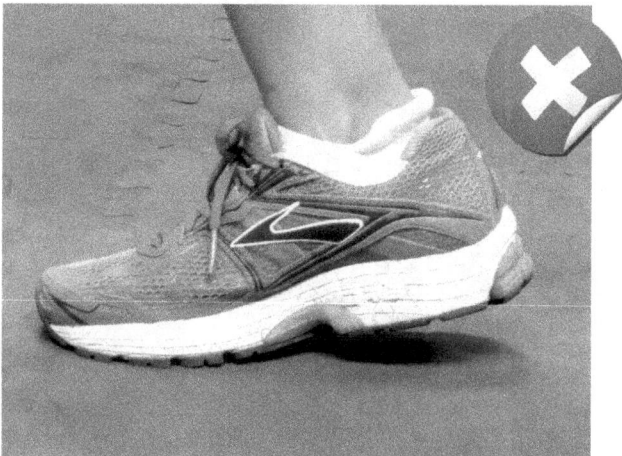

Fig. 2b: Weight skewed to the toes/ball of the foot results in knee pressure and pain.

- Does their pelvis shift laterally when they shift weight on to their front foot? This is best seen from either a front or posterior view (Fig. 3a and 3b).

Fig. 3a: Correct position; no pelvic shift. Distance between pole and hip is close to or equal to shoulder and pole.

Fig. 3b: Incorrect position; note the unequal distance between pole and hip, compared to shoulder and pole.

- Does their knee drift into a valgus position, which is a contributing factor towards Chondromalacia Patella and possible Medial Meniscus/ACL tears? Best seen from the front (Fig. 4a and 4b).

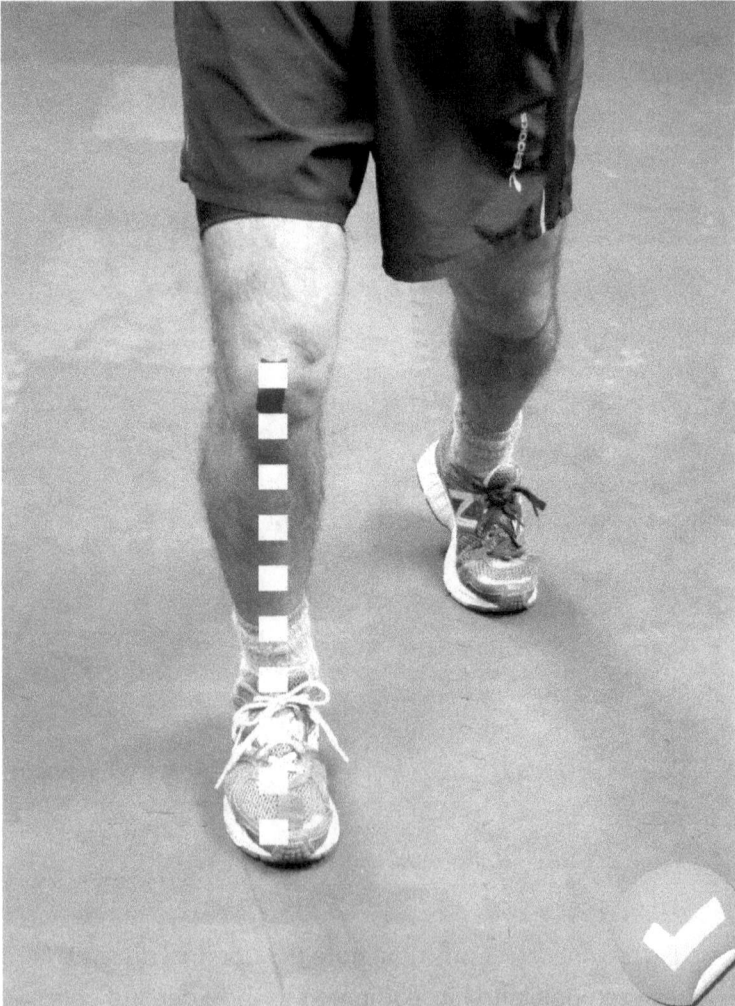

Fig. 4a: Correct position; knee stays directly vertical in line with foot.

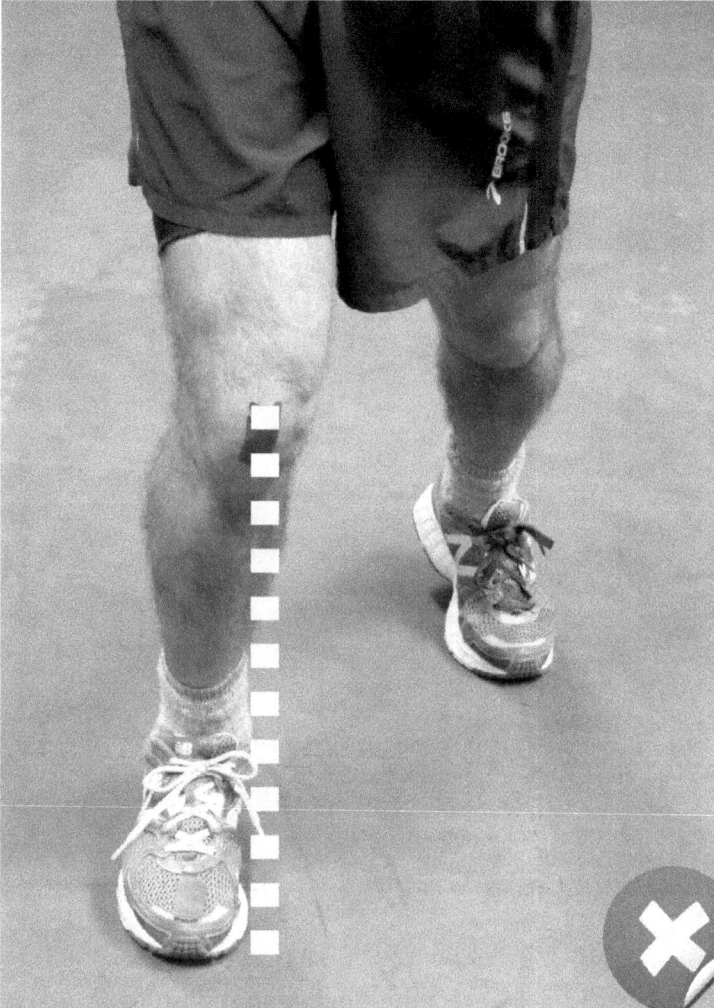

Fig. 4b: Incorrect position; knee drifts toward the center.

- Do they have upright posture? Slumped posture will effect the arm swing pattern, decrease respiratory capacity, shift the weight bearing onto the forefoot, shorten the stride, and potentially inhibit hamstring performance. A side view is best (Fig. 5a and 5b).

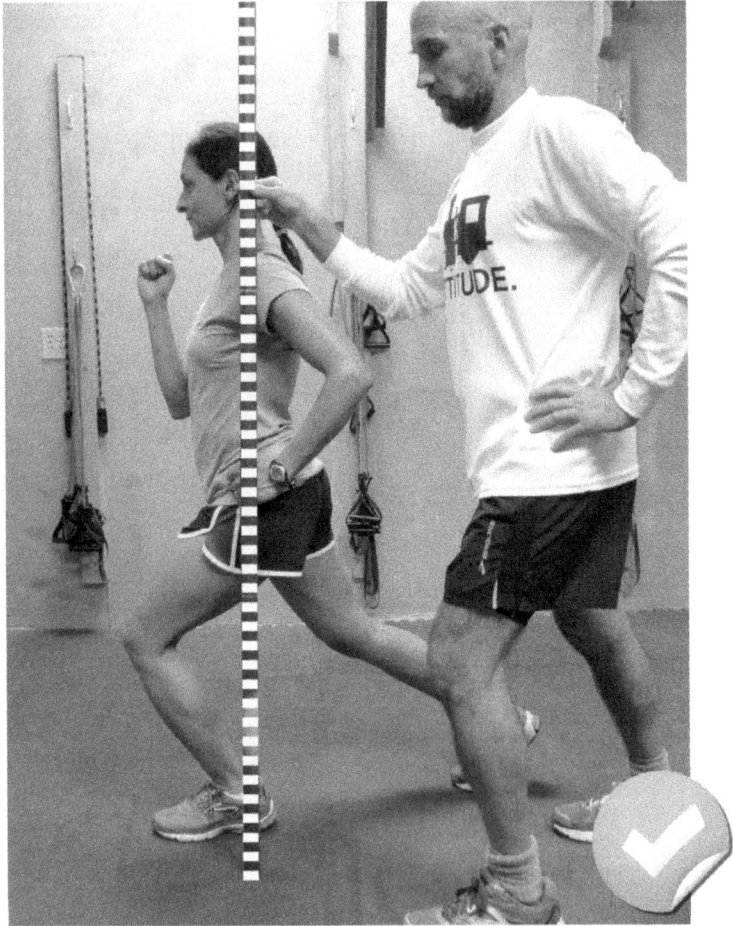

Fig. 5a: Correct position; upright posture.

Fig. 5b: Incorrect position: slumped posture
causes performance problems.

- Lastly, a very common issue in women athletes is the **triangle stance**. A front view is best (Fig. 6a and 6b).

Fig. 6a: Incorrect stance (triangle); unequal horizontal distance between knees and feet.

Fig. 6b: Correct stance; equal horizontal
distance between knees and feet.

Problem #1:
Center of Gravity over Base of Support

The most common issue here is that most athletes will stand with their CoG posterior to their base of support or weight bearing foot. In gait/run biomechanics language this would be the mid-stance phase. I prefer to call it the *acceptance* or *compression* phase, which makes it a much more dynamic phase compared to "mid-stance" phase which seems so passive. When the CoG is posterior to the base foot, the athlete tends to stiffen the leg on landing, which increases ballistic forces to the knee and hip, produces a mild braking effect and limits the potential for Stored Kinetic Energy (SKE) in the Posterior Kinetic Chain (PKC).

Fig. 7a: Sinking into the leg: Preloading, and Fig. 7b: Loading

THE FIX:

Teaching your athlete to flex the ankle and knee sufficiently and learning to *sink* into the leg as opposed to stiffening the leg. This will both decrease the impact/ potential injuries and improve their propulsion. This can be a very foreign concept to many athletes. However, once they accomplish it, they will feel more balanced, have better activation of the hamstring and gluteal muscles, and have less knee pain when running downhill.

PROBLEM #2:
WEIGHT DISTRIBUTION ON THE RUNNER'S FOOT

You will be amazed at how few athletes know how they are standing. This problem is many times intertwined with Problem #1. Overloading the forefoot will increase patellar pressure (complaints of knee pain with lunges, squats, and running) and decrease the ability to use the hamstring and gluteal muscles.

THE FIX:

Lots of cueing with a mirror and increasing athlete awareness of pressure on the knee and feeling their hamstrings activate. When it is corrected by solving Problem #1 the athlete will be able to self-correct by feel and eventually come to detect a proper landing compared to an improper landing or their old pattern.

Problem #3:
Lateral Pelvic Shift with Single-Leg Stand

In the medical profession, this is called a Trendelenburg gait. In the world of sports biomechanics it is a lateral pelvic shift and can be caused by either weak hip stabilizers or more often by the fact that the client has never learned how to activate them at this stage. The lateral shift in stance contributes to ITB problems, genu valgus, and inefficient tracking of the CoG for distance runners. The surprising thing is that this can even show up in athletes who perform many 'Monster Walk' drills with exercise bands, proving that just because we build up a muscle does not mean that it will work properly (i.e. have the correct neuromuscular pattern).

The Fix:

This is a tough one to fix and the best example is found on the website *The Gait Guys*. You have your athlete stand with 75% of their weight on the Left leg and with the pelvis level. Then slowly lower the Right side by doing an eccentric release of the Left Gluteus Medius. Once the pelvis is lowered, return to the level position by using a concentric contraction of the same Left Gluteus Medius. Be careful to watch for substitutions by the Right Quadratus Lumborum, or pushing up with the Left leg. If done correctly, the athlete will feel the Left Gluteus Medius contracting in a very small isolated area. This commonly requires some manual assistance to initiate (Fig. 9a, 9b, and 9c). We also recommend a bandwalk exercise (see pages 46 and 47).

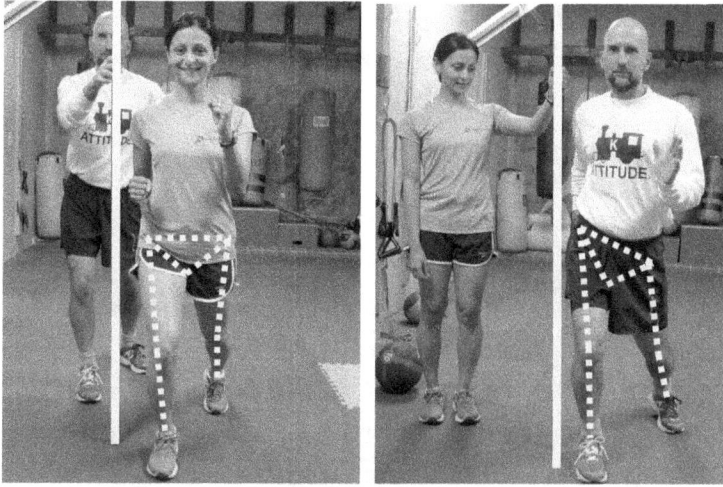

Fig. 8a: Correct position; no pelvic shift.
Fig. 8b: Incorrect position, pelvis not level.

Fig. 9a: Starting position with both legs
at same height and level pelvis.
Fig. 9b: Mid-exercise position with dropped
pelvis (Left leg stays straight).
Fig. 9c: Ending position.

Problem #4:
Knee Drift or Genu Valgus

This is a fancy term that describes the knee of the weight-bearing leg drifting towards the midline. This drift is the culprit behind complaints of knee pain with lunges, running downhill, foot pronation, ITB irritation, and it can be associated with Medial Meniscus/ ACL tears. Many high school and college teams already have a KLIP (Knee Ligament Injury Prevention) program in place. This is important because having a correct position is the basis of every part of the run program that follows.

The Fix:

Here you also want to strengthen and, even more importantly, teach the athlete kinesthetic awareness. Strengthening is similar to the fix for Problem #3 where we use an exercise program to build up the Gluteus Medius and other hip stabilizers. However, the most important aspect is to improve your athlete's ability to maintain proper position when running, jumping, and landing in order to avoid the complications that accompany this problem (Fig. 10a and 10b.). If you do not teach this kinesthetic awareness, it will not matter how much strengthening you do, as the athlete will revert to their old injury-prone habits when running. There are several very impressive teaching articles in the NSCA Research Journals with step-by-step training for athletes.

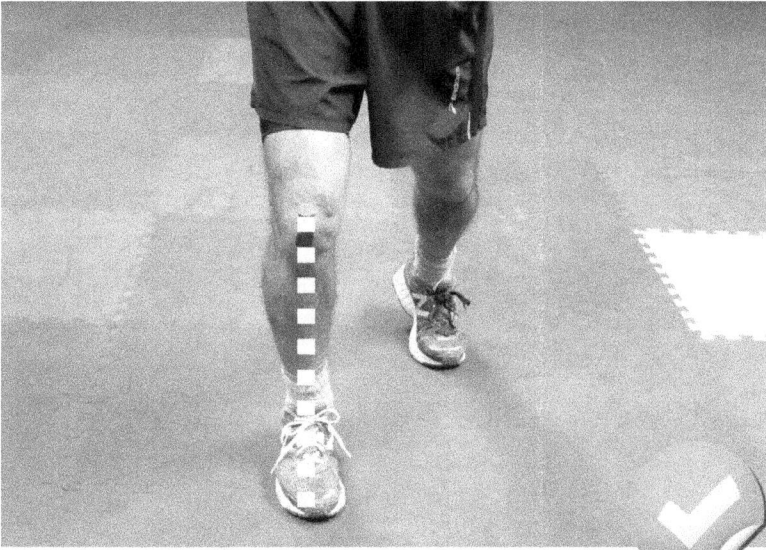

Fig. 10a: Correct position. Knee in line with second and third toe.

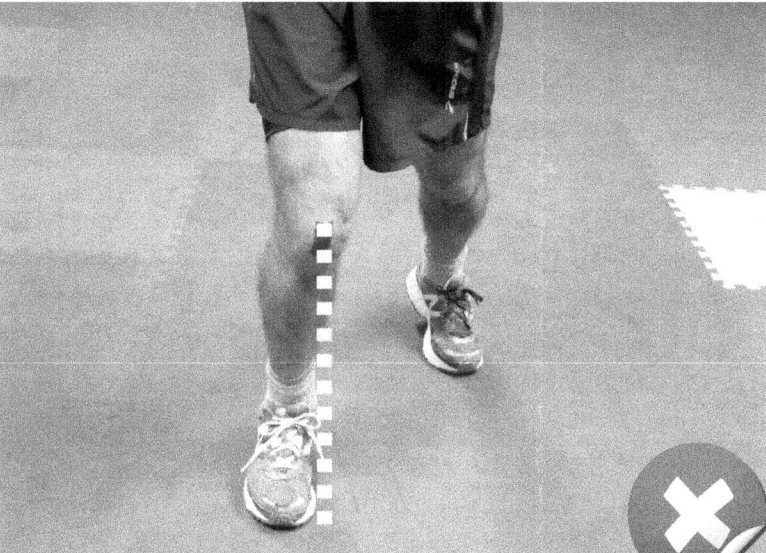

Fig. 10b: Incorrect position creates pronation at ankle and can tear the ACL/medial meniscus.

PROBLEM #5: POSTURE

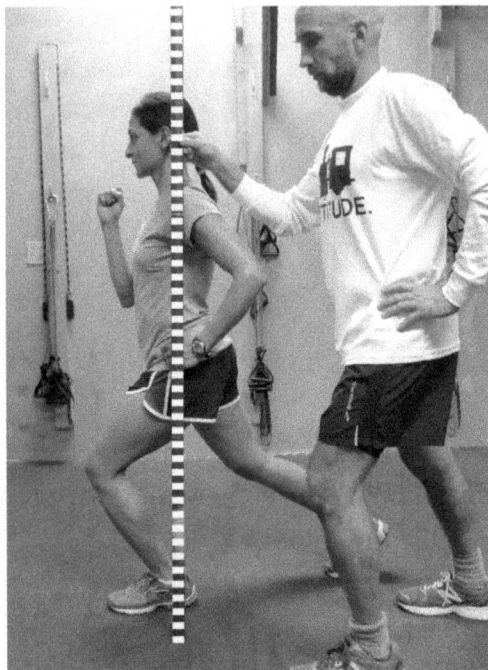

Fig. 11: Correct position; upright posture.

I know that many of you are thinking, "What the heck does posture have to do with running injuries?" The short answer is to remember that everything is connected, and if any part of the machine is out of plumb it will affect the rest of the machine.

- For starters, think of your spine/posture as the unit that is responsible for maintaining symmetry between the upper and lower halves of your body.

- Secondly, bad posture will inhibit your respiratory capacity which is not good for anyone, and especially runners. Talk to any singer/musician who has studied the Alexander Technique and they will attest to this.
- Thirdly, it will affect your arm-swing mechanics and decrease your running economy which makes you work harder.
- Next, that slumped posture will increase tension on the lumbar area as well as the hamstrings, inhibiting your stride pattern, which makes you slower.
- Lastly, it will reduce your stride by moving your CoG in front of your mid-point (observe the short shuffle of Parkinson's patients). Do you really want to run like that?

THE FIX:

There are many programs out there for posture. A good program should address both changing the structural limitations such as torso tape (Fig. 12a), foam rollers (Fig. 12b), posture devices (Fig. 12c) and, of course, should include a strengthening program of the targeted musculature. It is very important to make sure that your athlete has the structural flexibility to attain—and maintain—good upright posture. If your athlete does not have the structural ability to maintain good posture then all the verbal cueing will just lead to frustration on part of both the coach and the athlete. Once you have the structural flexibility and kinesthetic awareness, then it is time to start a strengthening program.

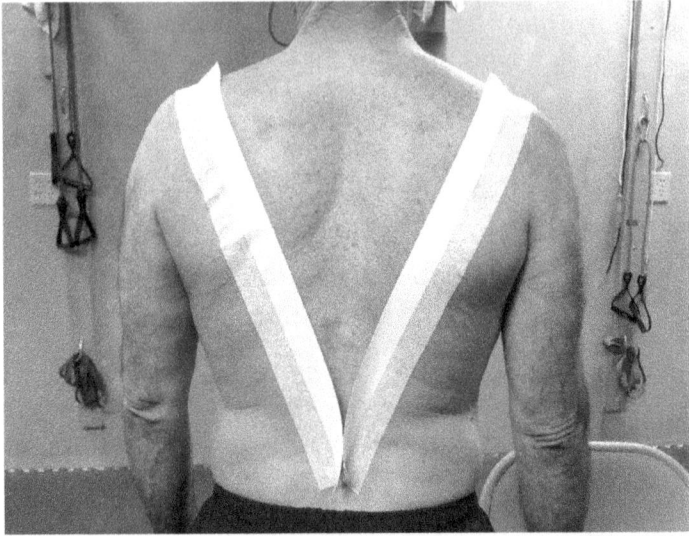

Fig. 12a: Torso tape.

Fig. 12b: Foam roller under the back to stretch.

Fig. 12c: Posture devices such as tubes attached with an elastic band around the lower back to give positive-pressure feedback at the spine and the back of the head.

Problem #6: Triangle Standing

I have seen this quite frequently with women athletes. It is also addressed in sports literature with KLIP programs. Triangle standing is when a client stands with their feet parallel and their knees are closer to each other (and commonly hyperextended) than their ankles, creating a virtual triangle. If you were to draw a line connecting the legs at the feet, that line should have the same length when drawn between the knees (Fig. 13a and 13b).

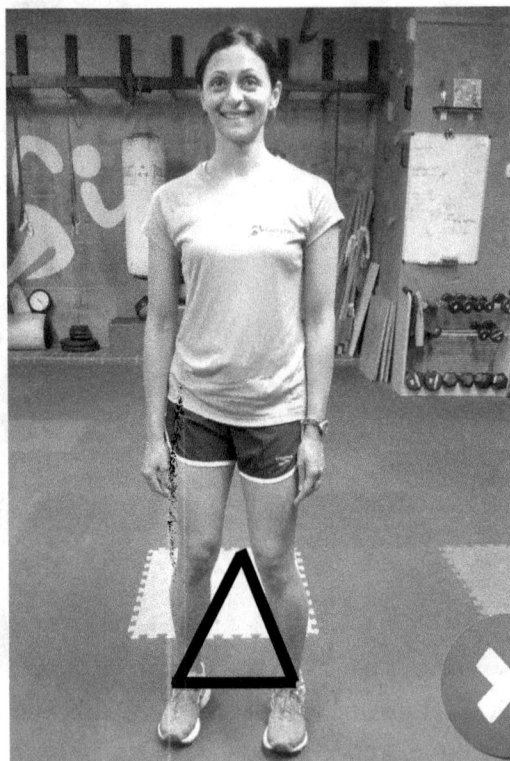

Fig. 13a: Incorrect stance (triangle); unequal horizontal distance between knees and feet.

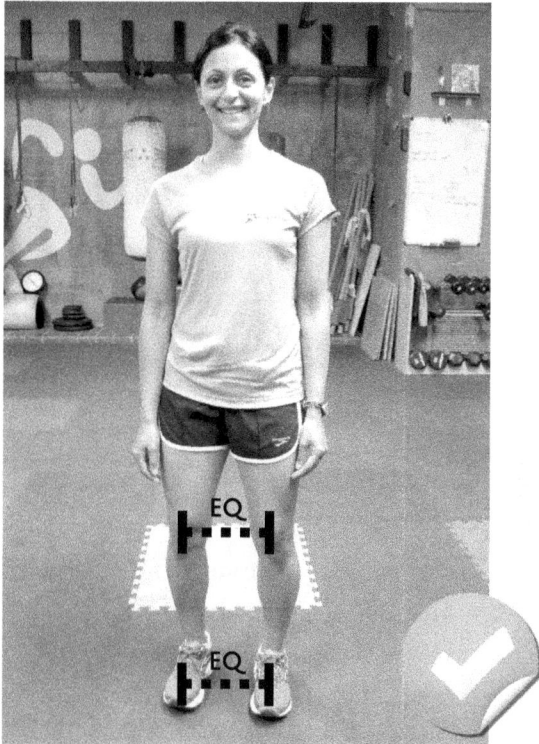

Fig. 13b: Correct stance; equal horizontal
distance between knees and feet.

THE FIX:

This is done with many of the same exercises as for Knee Valgus, as well as doing squats in front of a mirror while paying attention to leg positioning similar to a KLIP program. Initially the client will feel like she is standing very bow-legged, while in fact the tibias (shinbones) will be vertical and the kneecaps will line up perfectly over the second and third toe of the foot. Doing this correctly will decrease the chance of injury to the Medial Meniscus/ACL complex and reduce complaints of Chondromalacia Patella.

Chapter 2:
Biomechanics or
The Big Kahuna

Five-Part Stepping

The goal here is to develop a proper foot strike, weight transfer, and eventual push-off in a smooth, efficient, and linear pattern.

If done correctly, it will teach the client how to:

- run smoother (read *easier*) and faster.
- run with little to no vertical displacement.
- reduce the wear-and-tear factor significantly.

When I teach this to my clients, the most common feedback is "I feel like I was barely working yet I'm getting faster lap times." Or "I feel like I am running so low." This is because now they are no longer bouncing up and down (vertical displacement). The five steps are: Grab, Pull, Load, Go, and Reload. In this next section I explain the five steps in detail and add a number of specific exercises for each step.

STEP 1: GRAB

This describes the moment when the lead foot touches the ground and before the body weight is transferred. At this point the runner begins to actively pull both down and backwards with his foot. Dr. Michael Yessis in his book *Explosive Running* refers to this as "pawing". A very important aspect of this stage is for the runner to develop the sensation of being connected to the ground as if wearing spikes. My visual reference is a mountaineer who digs her ice axe into the frozen cliff in order to pull herself upwards or a canoeist who puts his paddle in the water in order to pull his canoe forward (Fig. 14a).

Fig. 14a: Diagram of Canoeist using his paddle to pull his canoe forward. A runner will dig /connect his foot to the ground in the same manner that a canoeist digs his paddle into the water in order to move ahead.

This is vastly different from the standard touch-the-ground motion that most recreational runners perform. The pawing action allows the runner to gain friction and therefore traction which in turn helps to activate the posterior kinetic chain much more efficiently than the conventional foot strike/touch-the-ground pattern.

WHY IS THIS SO IMPORTANT?

The Traction/Grab step improves the transfer of force between the foot and the ground. The biggest benefit of this action is that it produces a force vector (if done correctly) of the foot pulling down and backwards, which in turn propels the body forward in a linear direction. This is much more efficient and less injury producing than the traditional foot strike pattern.

There are a couple of ways to 'upload' this concept:

A). Actually wear track spikes and go for a slow walk/jog while focusing on the moment-of-grab. You should feel the sense of being connected and not just walking on-the-ground.

B). Stand in runner stance with a towel under the forefoot of your front foot. An exercise partner will grab and pull on the other half of the towel. This requires the runner to pull backwards (as if digging in with the front foot) and activate his posterior kinetic chain (Fig 14b).

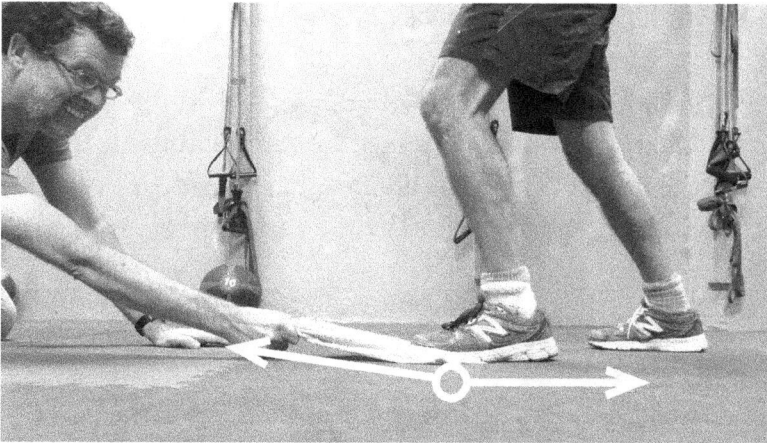

Fig. 14b: Vector lines show forward-pulling force applied by exercise partner and backward-pulling force of runner grabbing the towel with his front foot.

Once the client can maintain a good position (no genu valgus or lateral hip-shift) with this drill then we slowly add in the arm swing and the high-knee drill (see the Symmetry chapter).

STEP 2: PULL OR MOVE FROM THE CENTER (C.o.G)

In this section the runner begins to actively transfer his or her weight onto the stance/support leg. Here the 'AHA' moment comes from moving the body over the foot, which differs from the common idea of pulling the foot backwards. The concept here is of pulling the body forward while the foot acts as an anchor point. This can be compared to swimming when the lead hand will 'catch' and pull the body forward (elite swimmers probably do not think about their hands as the key point of their technique). Another visual analogy is sitting in a rolling office chair and pulling yourself forward with your feet. In this case the foot acts as an anchor that allows the posterior kinetic chain to pull the chair/body forward (Fig 15a-d).

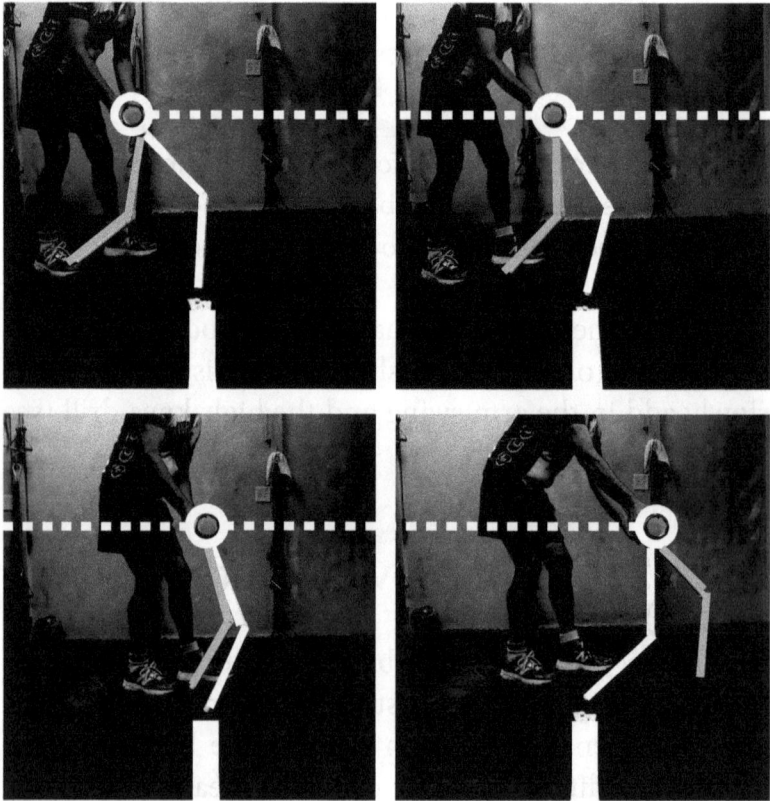

Fig. 15a-d: The white line on the ground marks the position of the grabbing foot. This shows that the body is moving over the foot, not the foot moving backwards.

I think that this technique represents a marked difference compared to many of the running fads out there that focus on the foot. All the fuss about barefoot, Pose, or Newton running is putting the cart before the horse. Starting with the fundamentals is very important as I see far too many runners using their upper body and arms to propel themselves at a huge energy cost. The main consideration is to transfer the CoG in a smooth and level fashion, and not by leaning the torso forward. I visualize being pulled by a rope attached to my belly button as I run (you can create your own visual). This is crucial when reducing vertical displacement and keeping the torso musculature relaxed.

Roll-Over Stepping Drill

This drill teaches the runner to move his CoG over the foot, again much like a swimmer pulls his body forward once he catches with his lead hand (see Fig. 15a-d above and Fig. 16a-e below).

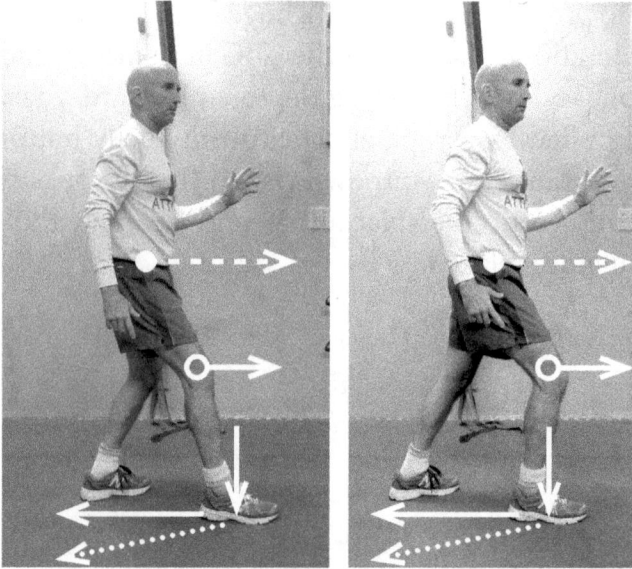

Fig. 16a and b: Vector lines indicate front foot pushing down and pulling backward (dotted line = resultant force) while CoG and knee move forward

Fig. 16c-e: The runner will focus on allowing the knee to keep shifting forward (think of the knee pulling the body) over the planted/gripping foot to the point that he 'falls forward' and the rear leg automatically swings forward to land as sort of safety mechanism for keeping the body upright. A big benefit of this drill is that the student will begin to feel their torso relax, and hopefully begin to feel like their torso is just along for the ride.

Steps 1 and 2 are almost simultaneous in real life, but taught as two distinct phases until the client can demonstrate good control/mastery of each technique.

STEP 3: LOAD THE SPRINGS/COMPRESSION

This is also referred to as the compression or weight-acceptance phase. At this point the previously mentioned grab with a proper alignment of hip and knee becomes very important. When those two variables are accomplished the runner can now safely 'load' the leg with his or her full body weight, without the risk of injury or loss of balance. Here the leg will actively flex at all three joints (ankle, knee, and hip). This allows the musculature, especially the calf muscles, to store kinetic energy (a big bonus). I like to think of your leg as a big spring being compressed before it springs back to full length while propelling you forward (Fig. 17a and 17b).

I believe that this is a big difference between what we do at Coach K Fitness and most traditional running schools: most foot-strike runners tend to land with a stiffened leg which does many bad things:

— it increases the chance for injury due to the increased impact force,
— limits the amount of stored kinetic energy,
— and has less activation of the PKC.

When my new clients finally 'get it' they talk about feeling like they can "run forever" as it feels so easy now.

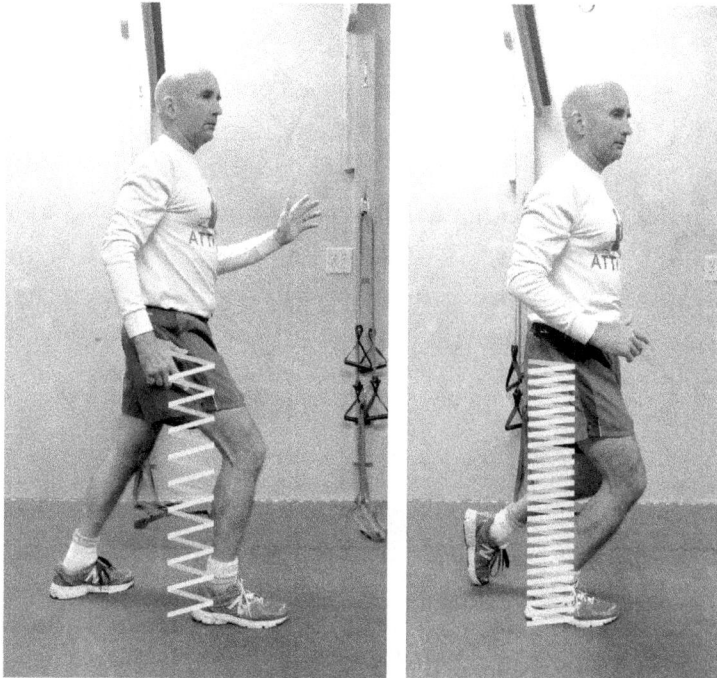

Fig. 17a: Preloading, and Fig. 17b: Loading

Following are a few exercises that will help you master this section as it does take a little bit of leg strength to control the loading phase:

Band Walking

This is important enough to have its own section. While Band Walking (Fig. 18a-d) is also one of the exercises used for controlling Lateral Hip sway, it is crucial for injury-free running. When these muscles are working properly, the runner can:

— maintain a level pelvis.
— change direction easily and safely, which is
    important in trail running and most sports.
— control knee drift, foot pronation, and all
    the problems associated with it.

We have changed the common method of band walking into a three-step process, which we think goes hand-in-hand with our five-part stepping technique, allowing for greater isolation and development of the hip stabilizers.

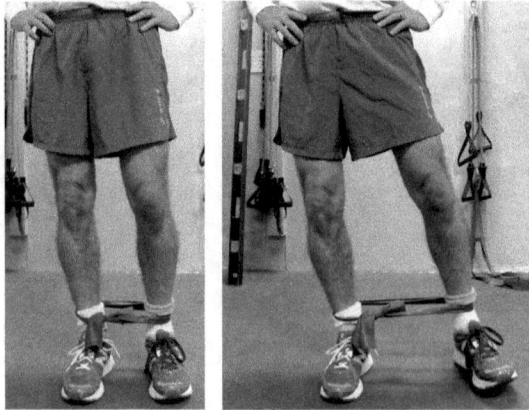

Fig. 18a: 1. Stand with feet parallel and shift weight to one leg;
Fig. 18b: 2. While keeping the weight on the support leg, move
the leading leg out to the side without moving the torso.
Think about leading with the knee and not the foot as this
will help prevent the dreaded triangle stance (see Fig 13a);

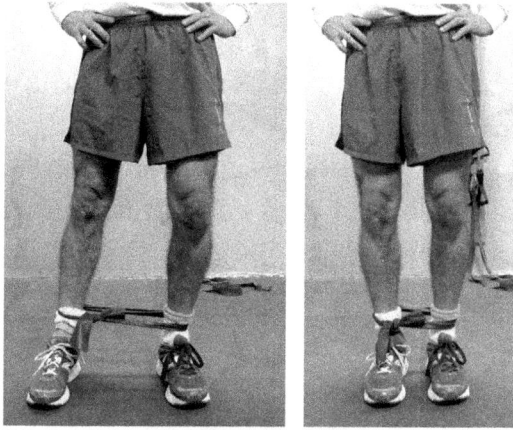

Fig. 18c: 3. Shift the torso and weight onto the lead leg while maintaining a vertical posture and non-triangle stance (see Fig. 13b); Fig. 18d: 4. Repeat steps 1-3 for a given distance and then return to the start with the other leg leading. If done correctly you will feel *significant* muscle work at the hips and almost nowhere else.

Hip Stability (HAM)

See lateral shift in Chapter 1: Screening for Basic Structural Components, pages 16 and 17.

While this may seem too simple, it is a very important aspect of running for both injury prevention and conservation of energy. We want all of our force to be going forward, not side to side. That side-to-side slide is great for fashion models walking down the runway but not for running.

Pendulum-Swing Drill

Have the athlete stand in Runner stance and shift all of his weight to the forefoot (same as Fig. 1a). While they are standing with good posture and CoG over the foot, ask them to swing the non-weight-bearing leg to the front as if taking a step, and then return to the starting point (Fig. 19a-c).

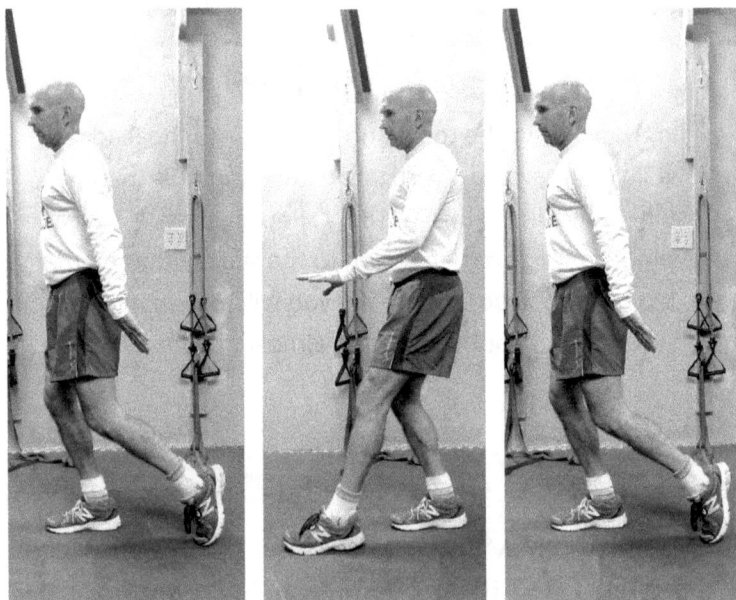

Fig. 19a: Start position of drill; Fig. 19b: Middle position of drill; Fig. 19c: End position of drill.

They should be able to maintain CoG over the base the foot, maintain posture, and knee alignment while swinging the free leg. If the athlete does demonstrate a problem with balance, trouble-shoot to find the exact cause, e.g. poor weight shift, weak hip stabilizers, weak ankles, etc. before starting an exercise program.

Balance Drill

Ankle exercises with a ball (Fig. 20a and 20b) will strengthen the Inversion/Eversion muscle groups of the ankle, and improve your ability to land securely on all surfaces. Again, the idea of any energy spent on correcting balance challenges and near falls is misspent energy that could be spent on forward propulsion. **This is important!**

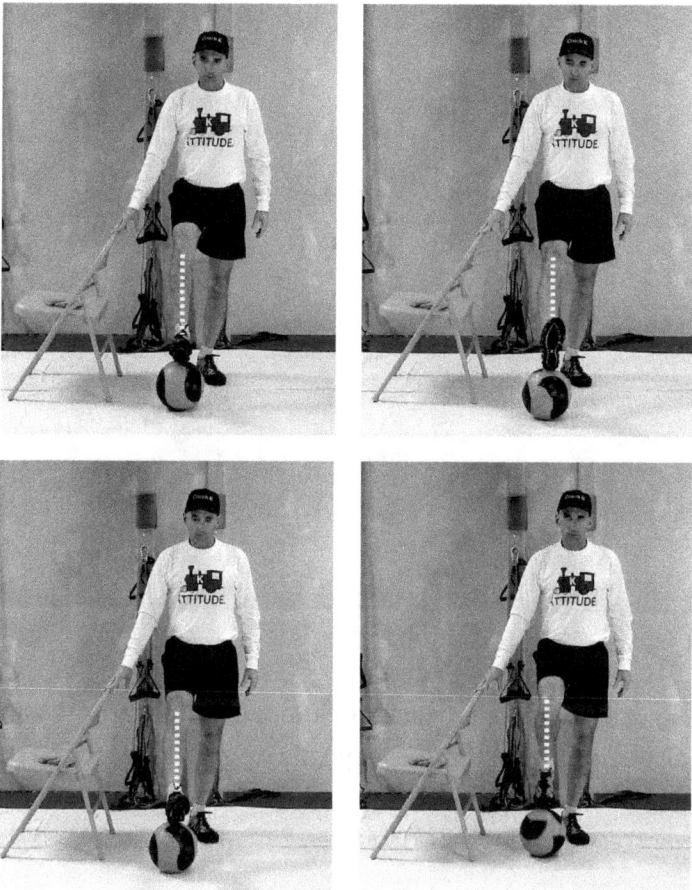

Fig. 20a: Stand with one foot on a ball. Roll ball straight back and forth (notice that the knee stays straight above the foot).

Anyone who has ever had an ankle sprain should do an in-depth program of both strengthening and proprioception training. The ligaments will not magically return to their pre-injury shape, the same as the dent in the side panel of your car will not magically fix itself.

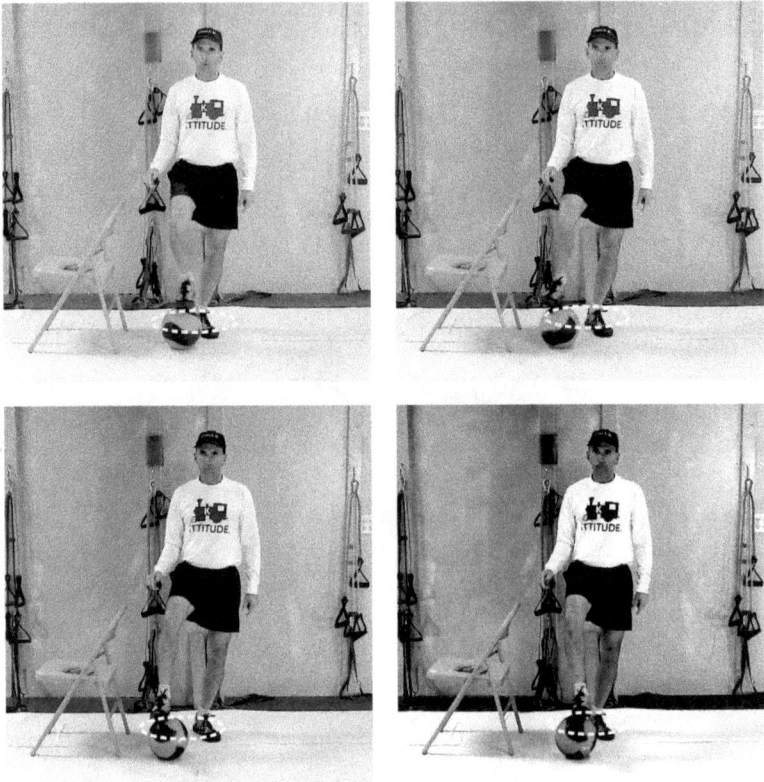

Fig. 20b: Roll a ball in circles to improve ankle strength and balance; note that there is very little weight being put on the ball from the rotating leg and foot. Do this exercise clockwise and counterclockwise (counterclockwise shown above).

One-Legged Squats

We love doing one-legged squats for two reasons. First, it is a great method for muscle balancing and not letting the dominant leg take over, as is common in usual squats, deadlifts, etc. Secondly, running is a one-legged activity. We need to train each leg to be able to work independently.

There are many different types of one-legged squats, and we suggest that you work with a certified trainer/ coach to make sure that you are doing them correctly. Or you can contact us for a training program that will match your current fitness level.

Step 4: Go

This is the topic that gets all the attention, but it is very dependent on the other three variables. At this point the three joints that have been in flexion during the compression phase and storing up kinetic energy will now rapidly go into extension and produce the force which drives the runner forward, and as a result it produces increased stride length. Here the timing of muscle firing is very important so that the resultant force vector is linear and not vertical in expression (Fig. 21). I like the comparison of how a paddle stroke in canoeing (see Fig. 14a) or a swim stroke will transition from a pull to a push once you're past the center point.

Fig. 21: Resultant force vector from rear foot pushing back propels athlete forward horizontally, not vertically.

Here we recommend the one-legged squats mentioned above, and lots of plyometrics as the force has to be delivered with considerable power in a very short amount of time if you want to run with speed. Some safe and easy types of plyometrics are skipping, rope jumping, bounding, squat jumps, and broad jumps. Please make sure that your technique is correct and consult a certified coach if you desire to use any higher level plyometric exercises.

Heel Raises

They are old school and very important. Think of your calf muscles as little booster rockets. Most runners merely shuffle along with very little push off, even those folks who practice the cadence system of counting steps per minute. While this is fairly efficient and has very little chance of injury (see the Bibliography section in the back of this book for Futterman's article on gait analysis), it is also very slow and boring. Learning to use your calf muscles will help to move you from the land of shufflers and joggers into the land of runners. Start with both feet up on a short 2x4, then push yourself straight up (Fig. 22a and 22b).

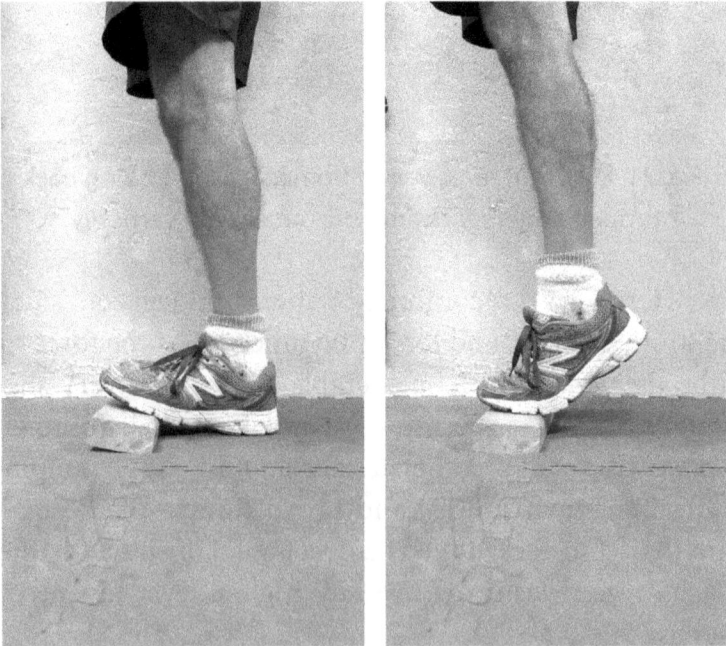

Fig. 22a: Starting position and Fig. 22b: Ending position

Remember to maintain a small amount of knee flexion. You should feel yourself going straight up and not forward. It is OK to touch a wall or some other support next to you for balance support. When you are able to consistently do these for one minute without stopping, progress to doing single leg heel raises (Fig 22c and 22d). Build those calf muscles as they will make you faster and help protect you from ankle injuries.

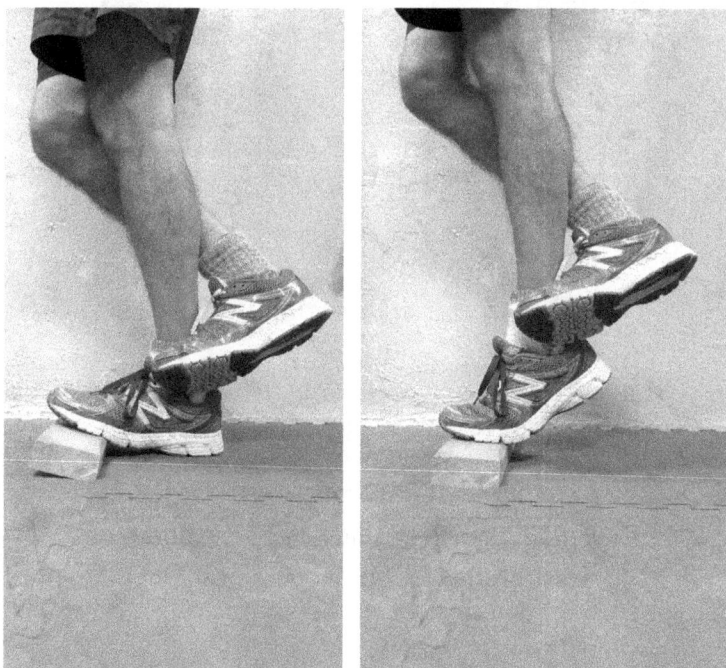

Fig. 22c: Starting position and Fig. 22d: Ending position

Make sure to keep the body vertical when pushing up (Fig. 23). Do not lean forward (Fig. 24).

Fig. 23: Correct position. Keep the body vertical and Fig. 24: Incorrect position.

Step 5: Reload

At this point, the runner has finished with his push-off/go and must now rapidly return the leg to starting position. Here is another triple-flexion moment of the ankle, knee, and hip. The faster that one can 'tuck' the leg during the return process, the better, since the work required to move a short lever arm through a set distance is less than moving a longer lever arm. Visually the whole run pattern from step 1-5 is very similar to the pattern used while riding a bicycle, even though the muscular recruitment pattern is so different (Fig. 25a and b).

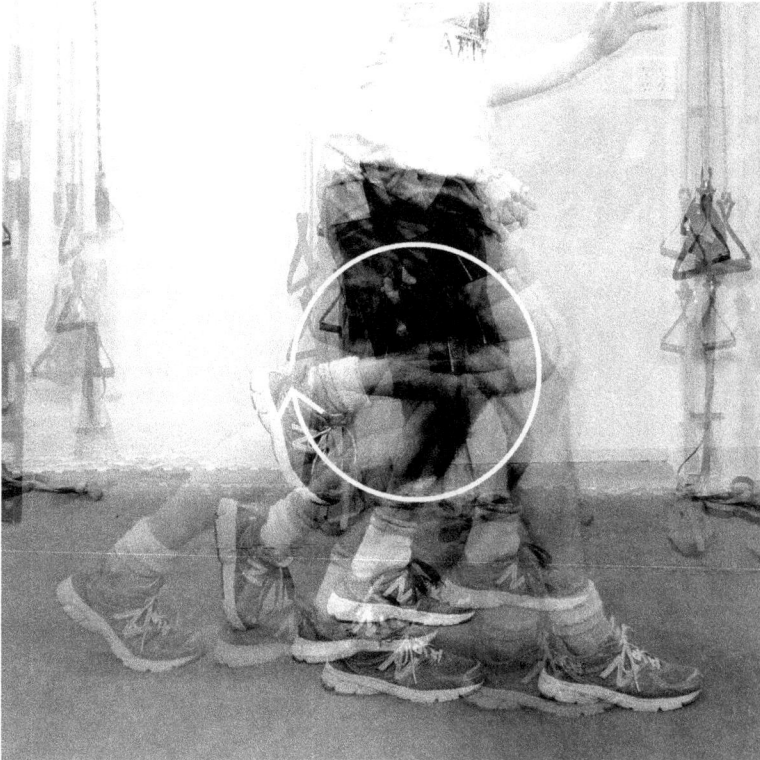

Fig. 25a: All Five Steps in one image: the overlaid circle shows the smooth movement of the legs, similar to riding a bicycle.

1. Grab **2. Pull** **3. Load**

Fig. 25b: All Five Steps in sequence

4. Go   **5. Reload**   1. Grab

59

CHAPTER 3:
SYMMETRY

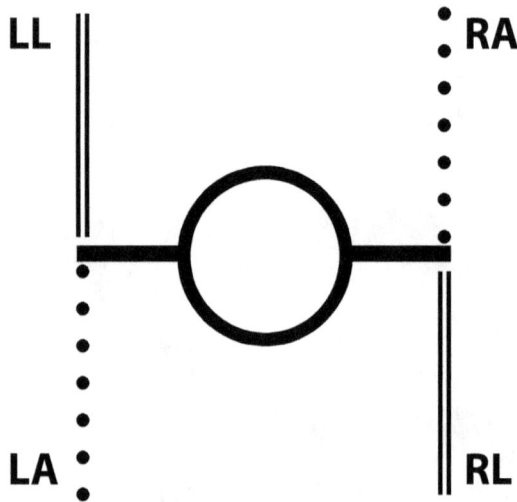

Fig. 26: Diagram of what a runner would look like from above. As you can see, everything balances out: LL (Left leg), RA (Right Arm), LA (Left Arm), RL (Right Leg)

Here is why the timing of arm swing and knee drive is so critical. In Fig. 27 you see the Right arm creating a forward motion with slight rotation from the Right to the midline, the Left Leg is creating a matching forward motion with slight rotation from the Left to the midline. When a runner maintains good posture, arm swing, and knee drive, the slight rotations will 'cancel' each other out and we are left with a Forward motion,

Runners with too much bad arm swing (see Fig. 31) or knee drift to the middle (see Fig. 28a and b) create a vector that pushes the trunk side to side much like riding your bike with wobbly handlebars.

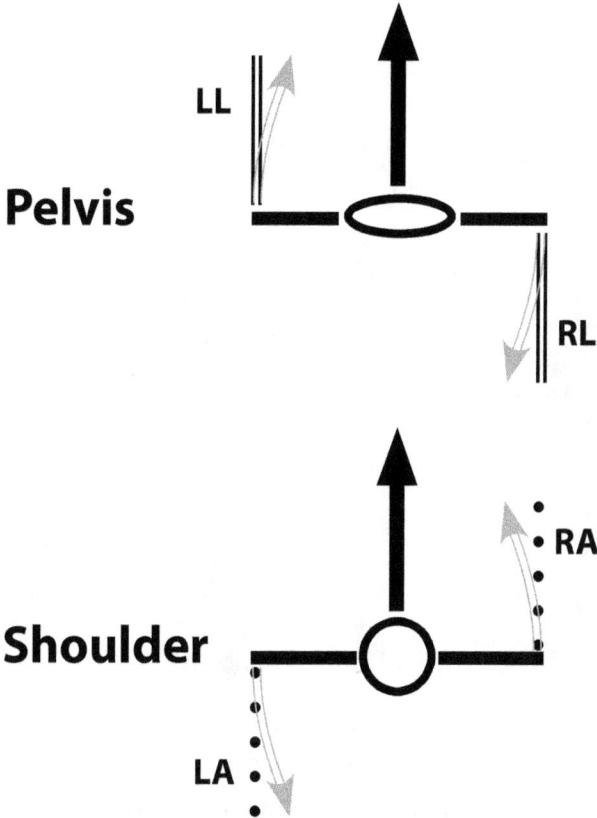

Fig. 27: Diagram showing canceling forces between shoulder and pelvis when running. Two large arrows indicate vectors of forward motion at shoulder and pelvis. Slightly rotating forces are shaded in small curved gray arrows; LL (Left leg), RA (Right Arm), LA (Left Arm), RL (Right Leg).

High-Knee Drill

Start with standing in place and lift knees only in alternating pattern. Watch for good alignment so that the knee comes up without any deviation to the middle (Fig 28a and b).

Fig. 28a: Correct position of knee
Fig. 28b: Incorrect position of knee
(rotation toward center of body)

Once they can demonstrate Step 1, we add matching arms and elbows. If you can have them stand in front of a mirror, put a piece of colored tape on the corresponding elbow and knee, then give the instruction that, when they lift that pair, they should be able to see the taped pieces simultaneously. Here the important thing is synchronicity of movement and good control, not how fast they can swing their arms (Fig. 28c).

Then we add one more progression. As they raise the knee-elbow pair, they will raise up on the stance leg (Fig. 28d) to the point of being on the ball of the foot/tip toe position. This creates the synergistic pattern of all flexion in the high-knee leg and all extension in the stance leg. This pattern will be used in actual running, especially for sprinters.

Fig. 28c: Correct running pattern; notice white tape
on knee and elbow to indicate synchronicity
Fig: 28d: Raising the body up on the stance leg and
standing on the ball of the foot/tip toe position

Arm Swing Drill

Here the athlete starts in mid-stance position with the arms in 90°-elbow flexion. She will focus on moving her elbows forward and backward in a rhythmic pattern while maintaining the 90° position. The idea is to learn to feel that the shoulder socket is the pivot point, similar to a pendulum (Fig. 29).

Fig. 29: Distance between elbow and CoG should be the same for both left and right arm. Maintain 90° between forearm and upper arm.

Once the athlete has the arm swing rhythm internalized, we add the torso control to the equation. Have a partner stand behind the runner with their hands on the runner's shoulder blades (Fig. 30). The runner is instructed to swing their arms while maintaining proper torso position (no motion). If their shoulder blade loses contact with the partner's hand, then they are twisting their torso (Fig. 31). Of course, you make sure that they are standing in correct posture, etc. according to Chapter 1.

Fig. 30: Partner lightly touches the runner's shoulder blades with the index fingers to provide positive feedback.

Fig. 31: Incorrect postures. Torso is twisted.

Lateral Shifting

Part of keeping good symmetry is being able to maintain the Center of Gravity and not having a 'leak' or lateral shift when doing full weight bearing on one leg. We recommend band walking and HAM exercises. (See illustrations under Step 3, pages 44-47)

Band Walking

(see Section above)

Runner's Bridge Progression

We start with the basic bridge exercise and tweak it. We teach the clients to initiate from their feet, not just 'shove their butt' up in the air. The client should start the exercise by pulling their feet into the floor to activate the hamstrings and, as they lift their pelvis, they should feel as if their knees are moving forward (from above the ankles and towards the toes) which in essence 'pulls' the butt up (Fig. 32). This creates a sense of ground force reaction and starts the connection between foot and pelvis which is very important. Now the client is learning to use the infamous posterior kinetic chain while decreasing stress on the patella (kneecap) and low back. Both of these are good things.

Fig. 32: Runner's Bridge, part 1: pull your butt
up by pulling their feet into the floor.

Once they can perform this correctly and consistently, we move on to single leg bridge and then alternating leg bridging in order to mimic the dynamics of running, which is a one-legged activity (Fig. 33).

Fig. 33: Runner's Bridge, part 2: single leg and alternate leg lifting mimics the dynamics of running.

Now we add in the arms to the bridging pattern. We feel that this is an important aspect that is all too often overlooked. The client starts with the arms in 90°-elbow flexion by their side. Then as he pushes down with the Right leg they push down with the Left elbow and lift the Right elbow to match the lifting Left knee (Fig. 34).

Fig. 34: Runner's Bridge, part 3: add the arms to the drill.

If done correctly, the client will look as if they are running while laying on their back. We perform this until the client can demonstrate a smooth and clean pattern, and is able to start/stop and resume a correct rhythm with no problem. The goal is to establish the neurological network for arm/leg swing and have it so ingrained that the client can now shift their focus to other aspects of running and not lose their rhythm.

Pendulum Swing Drill

(see Section above)

Posture/Core

We've written quite a bit about posture in the Screening Chapter, and would like to add a few comments:

'Duck Butt' Running

Here the runner has a fairly straight spine compared to the slumped-over runner. However, they lean the torso forward and compensate with pushing their butt backwards behind the plumb line (Fig. 35). This is perhaps worse than the forward slumped posture, because now you have two areas to fix. In this case the runner is not only shortening their stride by having the plumb line land over the forefoot, but the pelvis, being pushed behind the midline, severely limits any push off/go. Duck Butt runners will cruise along with a tiny stride pattern and little speed and yet inflict lots of stress on their feet.

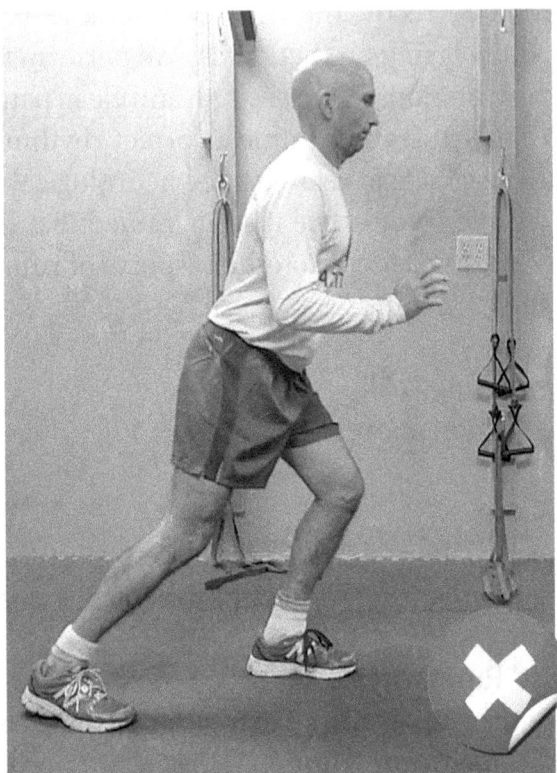

Fig. 35: Incorrect posture; 'duck butt' stance

Slumped Posture Running

Here the pelvis is over the feet but the torso is slumped forward (Fig. 35 and 36). This moves the vertical plumb line over the forefoot which makes it feel as if you are going to fall forward. As a result the runner ends up taking very short and inefficient strides in a constant battle not to tip over. This puts much more stress on the feet as there is no compression to absorb the impact of landing, and running in this position will also increase the stress on your neck and lower back.

Fig. 36: Incorrect, slumped posture

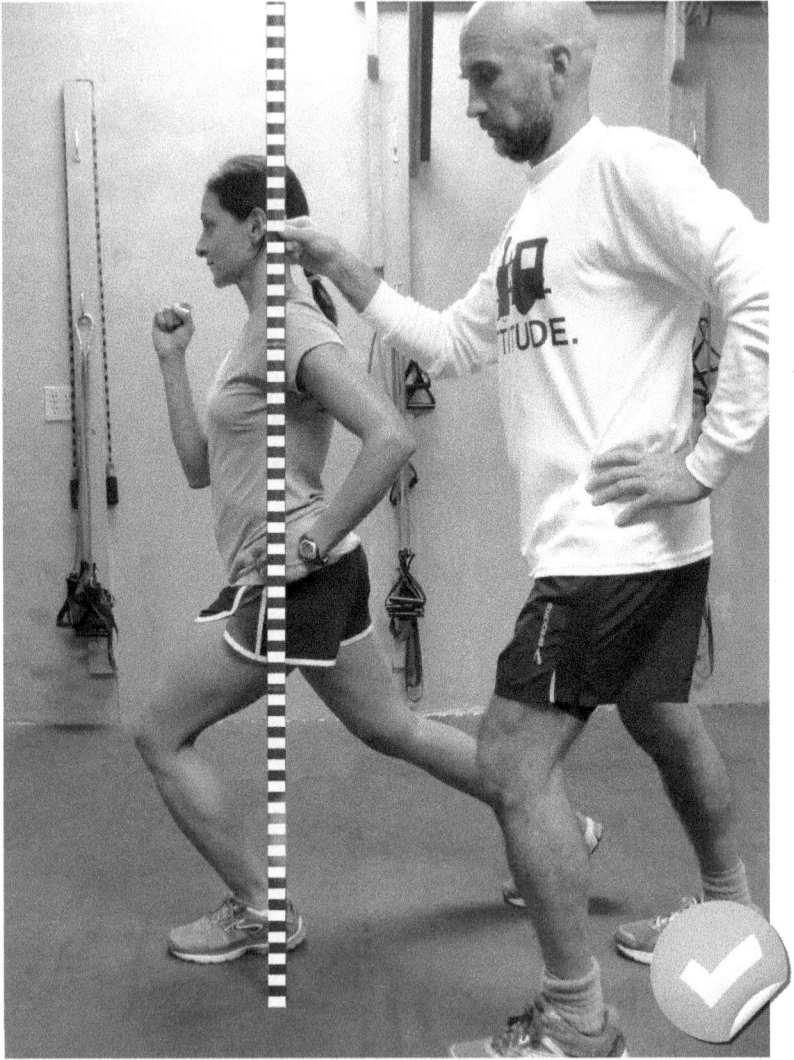

Fig. 37: Correct posture

Besides the exercises that were recommended in the Screening Chapter, I use the following with all my clients.

Scapula Progression

We believe in spending time in teaching the client how to activate and control their shoulder blades. This is important for several reasons. A good runner is able to maintain their shoulders in good posture and move their arms independently. When the arms and shoulders are pumping or swinging together, instead of using an independent arm swing, they create torso rotation which is very inefficient and a significant cause of the dreaded flying ponytails.

Start with the client standing in basic runner stance facing a wall equipped with pulleys or cables (Fig. 38a-d). They will hold the cable with arms straight and shoulders rounded (abducted) for the start position (Fig. 38a), then slowly pull (adduct/retract) the scapula with attention given to not flexing the elbows, as this will change the movement focus (Fig. 38b and Fig. 38c).

When they demonstrate good control with both arms, i.e. no substitution with lumbar extension, we expand on the drill by using just one shoulder at a time, followed by alternating shoulders. Next in the progression is to bring in the elbow after the shoulder, which tightens up all the upper back muscles. Then, while holding the shoulders in 'pull-back position', slowly let one arm come back into extension (Fig. 38d). This usually requires the client to focus on two opposing muscle actions e.g. pull the shoulder back and reach forward with the arm. We will alternate left and right to incorporate the same neurological sequence as running.

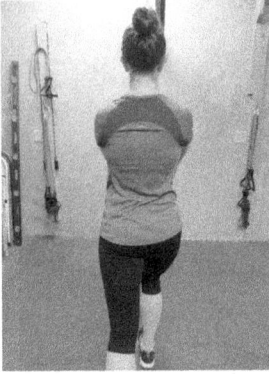

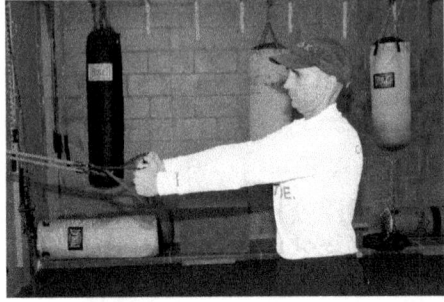

Fig. 38a: Start position of drill, back and side views

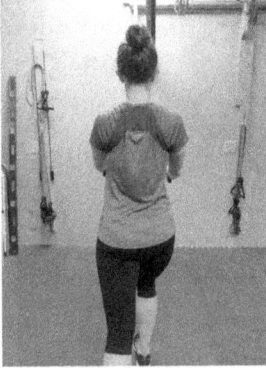

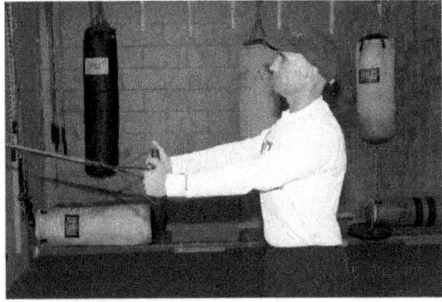

Fig. 38b: Mid position of drill, back and side views.

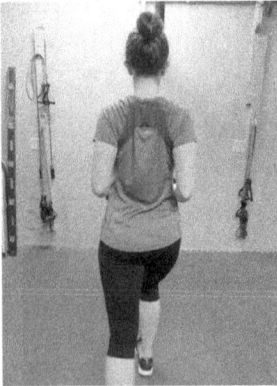

Fig. 38c: End position of drill, back and side views.

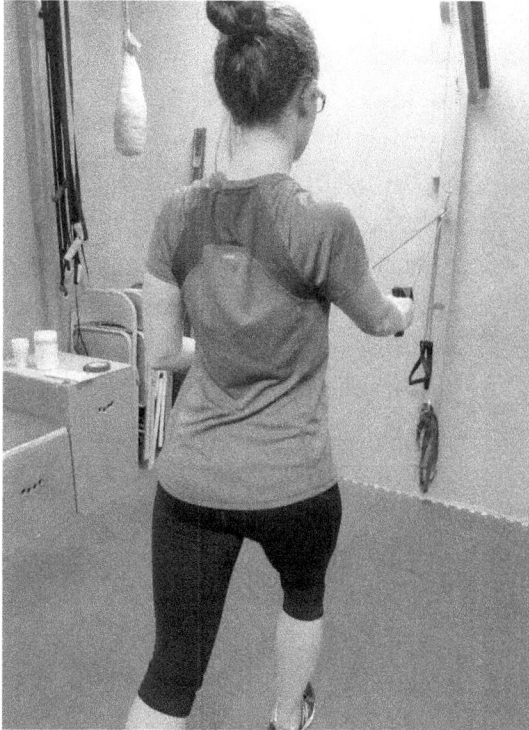

Fig. 38d: Squeeze the shoulder blades
with alternate arm positions.

Chapter 4: Core

Core strength is important as your core serves as both the anchor or foundation for your leg musculature and also controls torso posture. Without a strong core your posture quickly deteriorates and you look like those runners at the back of the pack struggling just to finish.

We suggest doing both integrated core exercises as well as isometric type exercises like planks or Bunkie test drills. Running is not a static activity, so we need to teach the core muscles how to respond and maintain control while the extremities are all moving separately. You can start with simple planks or sit ups to build a solid base. Then progress to the Bunkie test series and integrated core drills to develop a stronger and more functional core. Following is a list of three fundamental core exercises.

A. Janda Core Progression

This exercise comes from one of my favorite mentors, Dr. Vladimir Janda. (Fig. 39a-b).

Fig. 39a: Janda Core Progression; getting into position.

Fig. 39b: Janda Core Progression sequence: start, middle, and finish positions. Here the goal is to control the lumbar position on the mat while moving the legs. The stress imparted to the body is similar to keeping the torso upright while running.

B. Mat Drill with Arm/Leg Circles

Again, this is an integrated core, as the client will focus on keeping his/her lumbar area on the mat while simultaneously moving the diagonally opposite arm and leg in a circle (Fig 40). We do this because it mimics the stress of running.

Fig. 40: Sequence of diagonally opposite arm-and-leg motion to simulate the stress of running on a mat.

C. Stand with Modified Windmills

We do this drill to help with rotational control. The plan here is to focus on keeping your torso stationary and not twisting while you move your arms front/back in rhythmic pattern (Fig. 41a-c). We suggest starting slowly with an easy weight and gradually increasing the speed and weight as you improve. The focus is core stability, not arm strength.

Fig. 41a: Start position of drill.
Fig. 41b: Mid position of drill.
Fig. 41c: End position of drill.

CHAPTER 5:
BUILD THE ENGINE

Once the basic skill set is developed then it is time to build strength for both injury prevention and improved performance. Here is where many coaches will have big variations of opinion. Many traditional track coaches (and runners) believe that strength training is only done by running hills or stadium bleachers, and they have disdain for any program that involves weight training, as they fear it will make them big, bulky, and slow. Fortunately this is not true. For most recreational runners a well-organized strength program with proper technique can replace the daily short runs that are done to 'toughen up' the legs. In the 'old days' the daily runs served two purposes.

We build muscle and tendon tissue strength to prevent tears (see Wolff's Law from Wikipedia). This can be replaced by a good strength program, and for the runner with time constraints or bad weather problems being able to work out in gym at convenient times is a blessing. And there is research that shows that appropriate strength programs are a great way to improve running performance (See Livingstone reference on page 111).

Lunges

Begin in kneel position (Fig. 42a). Cues are to 'grab' with the foot, feel the CoG shift forward (Fig. 42b), and then use the PKC to pull forward and up (Fig. 42c). If you watch the pelvis, it is traveling in more of a 45° line as opposed to a more vertical line used in standard type lunges. The important thing here is to emphasize feeling the grab-with-the-foot motion and then pulling the CoG forward, otherwise the client will tend to use the quads as a primary mover.

Fig. 42a: Start position of lunge drill;
Fig. 42b: Middle position of lunge drill. CoG shifts forward;
Fig. 42c: Final position of lunge drill.

One-Legged Squats

There are many types of single-leg squat exercises that are good for building strength and balance such as the Bulgarian squat, lunges with rear foot on ball, etc. Please check with a certified coach to find one that works for you to make sure that you are doing them correctly (or contact us). I prefer single-leg exercises as it promotes muscle balancing and fits the idea of running as a one-legged activity. A good example can be found in an article by Joel Bergeron called "Hamstring Training for Injury Prevention" in *NSCA Coach* Vol. 2, Issue 2. pages 24-30.

Stadium Workouts

I have come to like doing stadium workouts, with a small caveat. Make sure you are using correct technique and know exactly what you are trying to accomplish. I have found that walking up the bleacher or doing big steps to be a sort of lunge-on-steroids. Make sure that your technique is correct so that you don't injure your knees. This will really improve strength for your PKC. All the other odd things like side-stepping over bleachers, walking or running backwards on ramps, etc. are just 'odd things', in my opinion, and should be avoided.

Tire Drag

The tire-drag drill or weighted sled is a very old-school approach for building leg strength in athletes (Fig 43). I like it because it builds muscle in the same neuromuscular firing pattern as running, compared to doing squats, deadlifts, etc. which just build muscle. I really like tire-drag training, as it can help me train for hills/mountain running while living in Florida. I believe that a one-mile workout produces a training stimulus to several miles unloaded. And with a good coach it can be incorporated into an amazing speed program.

Walking or running with a tire or weight sled will improve your 'levelness'. Having a weight sled or tire attached to a belt around your waist will make you have to pull from your center, and it is a great way to get rid of that 'bouncy' run, or vertical displacement (in scientific terms). Make sure to only use a tire that weighs about 10-15% of your bodyweight so that you do not develop over-leaning or other bad-posture habits.

Fig. 43: Tire-drag drill in action.

Runner Pushups

This is a rare arm and upper-body exercise. I prefer doing what I call a 'Runner Pushup', compared to the conventional style pushup, for two reasons (Fig. 44a-c). First, they teach the client to keep their elbows close to the body, which is important for symmetry.

Secondly, they focus on building triceps strength which is a very much overlooked aspect of running. I didn't realize this until I read Dr. Yessis' book *Explosive Running*. Most USATF Coaches just talk about how to drive the elbows forward. We train our runners to develop a neurological pattern to connect shoulder extension and hip extension of the appropriate arm and leg pair for improved propulsion. From that perspective runner pushups are very comparable to Nordic skiing.

Fig. 44a: Conventional pushup with arms moved away from the torso; Fig. 44b: Runner pushup, starting position. Notice how the arms are kept close to the torso; Fig. 44c: Runner pushup, finish position. Arms stay close to the torso.

Chair Squats

This is one of the few two-leg drills that we use, and it is a very safe exercise for beginners to build their leg strength. They start in a sitting position while facing a mirror (Fig. 45a-d). The goal is to monitor their legs and keep them from drifting into the valgus position during the come-to-stand or return-to-sit portion of the drill. When they have the basic exercise, they can progress to holding a weight or loaded backpack, and then progress to one-legged drills.

Fig. 45a: Chair squat, start position;
Fig. 45b: Chair squat middle position, incorrect posture

Fig. 45c: Chair squat, final position;
Fig. 45d: Chair squat with weight.

The intention of this book is to teach you proper biomechanics; it is not an indepth conditioning/training manual. We have provided some drills/exercises so that you will have the strength/muscle control needed to perform these biomechanics properly.

We will be glad to help you design an appropriate conditioning program for your training level and desired goals.

Chapter 6:
Flexibility

Ido not spend as much time working on flexibility as I do the above structural areas. I have coached runners with terrible flexibility and yet they do very well. Whereas, I have seen folks who do quite a bit of yoga and stretching not do so well and be prone to injuries. I will look at ITB flexibility and piriformis tightness briefly in the early stages and otherwise ignore it unless the client has an injury complaint (see Chapter 8, pages 97-100). However, I do like to work on tight hip flexors using the half-kneel stretch (Fig. 46) as so many people spend a large percentage of their day sitting while working on the computer, driving their car or watching TV. With the half-kneel stretch it is important to contract the core muscles and perform a posterior pelvic tilt. This should produce a slight stretch sensation along the front of the thigh and should tighten up the gluteus muscles.

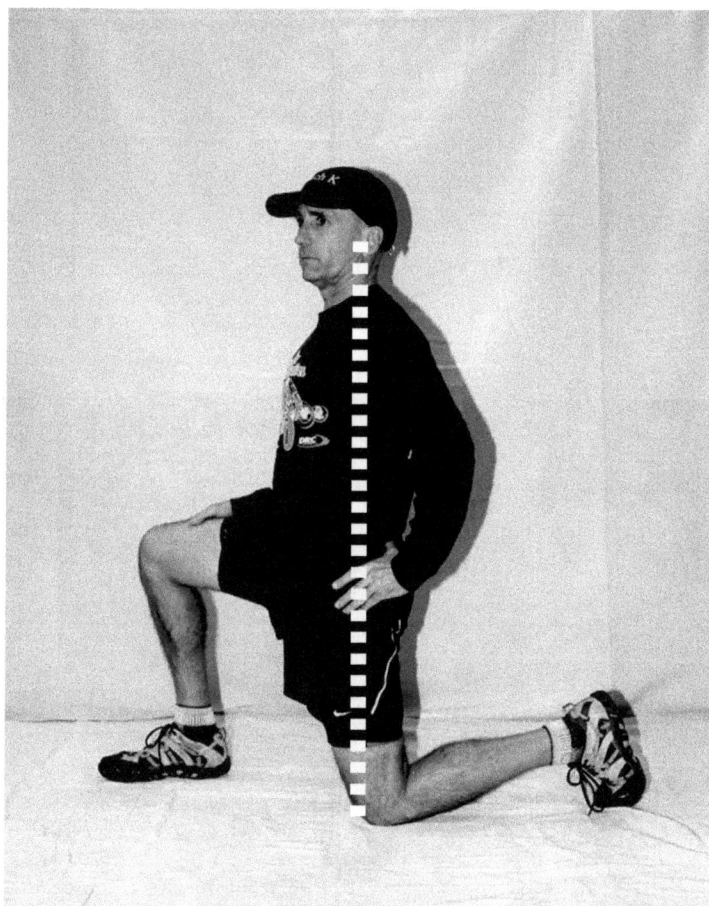

Fig. 46: Half kneel position. Make sure to keep an upright posture and a tight core. Use a posterior pelvic tilt to stretch the tight hip flexors. Do not lean back with your shoulders. Remember to keep good posture, and avoid the urge to lean forward.

Chapter 7:
Speed or Distance

Once runners get to the point of feeling comfortable and confident with their running skills, they hit the famous conundrum: run for distance or run for speed. This seems to be the big question for runners. I know I used to think that it was an either/or choice. You were either a distance runner or one of the 'speed guys'. Now I realize that this is no longer true. With a little planning it is possible to work on both areas as they each have their own benefits. We will talk about how these very different goals can be blended. Distance running for a speed athlete promotes running economy, and much like playing a piece of music over and over, it goes from initially playing by rote to eventually feeling the music.

The standard rule of thumb is to increase distance by 10% a week or whenever the current route starts to become comfortable. For those who want to train for bigger distance but lack the time in a given day, we start to use back-to-back runs. If you run ten miles on Monday and then ten miles on Tuesday, you get a training effect similar to running all twenty miles in one day.

I like to add an indoor strength or plyometric session in the mornings as a substitute for short runs and get the same training effect. Remember, there are many ways to skin a cat. Having a knowledgeable coach (you can contact us) is very helpful for setting up a training program.

For you distance runners, research has shown that speed drills will improve neuromuscular firing patterns, which can help make a distance runner more efficient. And for distance runners running economy is critical. Remember to be cautious with adding speed workouts to your program. Speed produces much more torque and muscle tension and can result in muscle tears which mean no running for a while. I would recommend starting with very short distance sprints and doing several sets. Do not work to fatigue!

We do sets of three, then have a short recovery period and then perform another set of three. We will continue this pattern until we notice a drop in our speed that does not return after the recovery period. This is not about endurance, but running at our best speed. So it is better to stop and wait until the next speed session instead of trying to do another set slower.

Speed can be broken down into a simple formula:

Cadence x **Stride Length** x **Ground Force Reaction** (GFR) x **Deceleration** (lack of speed)

Cadence

It has been my experience that most runners start with improving their cadence to the 'Holy Grail of 180 contacts/minute'. This is fairly easy to accomplish: practice, but do not get hung up on it. Some runners get too OCD about it. Just run at what is good for you.

Stride Length

This is determined to a large degree by genetics. A taller runner is going to have a longer stride length than a shorter runner, if they have equal GFR. Novice runners make the mistake of trying to increase stride length by over-reaching with their lead foot. This is very bad and will both slow you down and increase your chance of injury. The proper way to increase your stride length is by improving your GFR.

Ground Force Reaction (GFR)

GFR is Ground Force Reaction, a buzz word to describe how much power or force you are applying to the ground when your foot pushes off. This is simple Newtonian physics of "every force will apply an equal and opposite force". So the harder you push the ground, the harder the ground pushes you forward. A bigger push means bigger stride length and speed (see the chart in Keith Livingstone's book *Healthy Intelligent Training* on page 180).

This takes us back to the chapters on strength and plyometrics. Stronger legs have a stronger push. And old-fashioned sprints are another great way for developing a better GFR. When the muscles are forced to work faster they become more efficient (hopefully the baseline technique is good) and have a resulting stronger push.

Deceleration

This is a commonly overlooked area in the world of running. When I first received my Track and Field Coaching Certification, I remember hearing the old adage about sprinters: "It isn't about who accelerates faster, it is more about who doesn't slow down at the end." This is more about improving your cardio capacity than leg strength. The two go hand in hand for developing what we call 'speed endurance'. This requires throwing in some endurance building blocks in your training schedule. Personally, I like to make a weekly schedule with two to three strength days, one to two speed/plyometric and one long-run day.

The intention of this book is to teach you proper biomechanics; it is not an indepth conditioning/training manual. We have provided some drills/exercises so that you will have the strength/muscle control needed to perform these biomechanics properly.

We will be glad to help you design an appropriate conditioning program for your training level and desired goals.

Chapter 8:
Recovery

Compression Socks

There is quite a bit of research available today that documents the effectiveness of compression socks or other garments for recovery from training and competition (Fig. 47). I like to take a pre-emptive approach and wear compression gear during my big runs or stressful training events. I believe that wearing the compression gear will minimize the muscle tears or bone stress and promote better circulation. So if all this is happening during the run, then there is less need for a recovery session. And over the years I have seen many new runners get relief from shin splints by wearing compression socks.

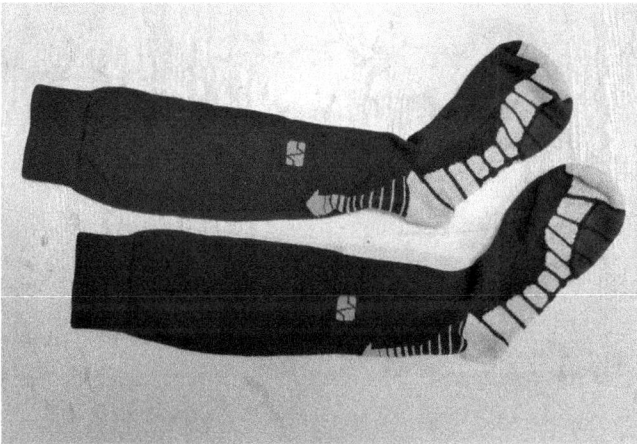

Fig. 47: Typical compression socks available commercially

Roller Pins

I have found these to be a great tool for achy muscles and shin splints (Fig. 48). The classic wooden roller pin is a very cost effective substitute for those long roller-massage devices found in stores. Be advised that rolling the achy area with sufficient pressure will be somewhat uncomfortable but it will produce amazing results. We recommend that you have someone else do the rolling, as most people fail to apply enough pressure.

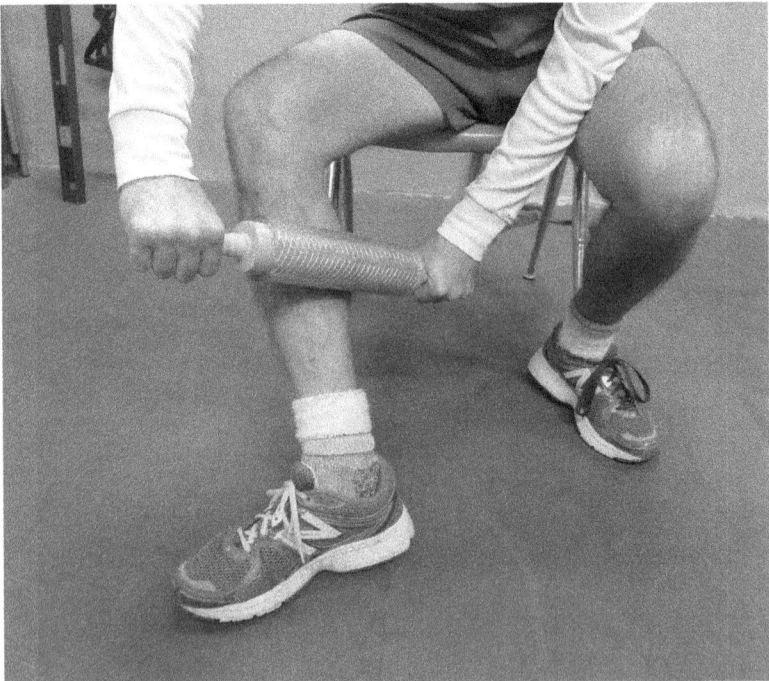

Fig. 48: Proper roller pin application

Nutrition

Beware the fads and glucose-starving diets. I strongly believe in just eating real food (organic if possible) and avoiding all those supplements and fads that are supposed to do amazing things. Nothing takes the place of consistent hard work. Take non-steroidal anti-inflammatory drugs (NSAIDs) only in limited doses. If you find that you are taking NSAIDs on a consistent basis, then you should get your running technique or training program evaluated by a certified coach.

Injuries
1. Iliotibial Band (ITB)

This is a very common injury in new runners when they bump up their mileage or start a new speed program. The complaint is of hip pain during the run and sometimes afterwards. Sometimes the athlete will have pain on the lateral aspect of the knee as that is the insertion point. I have found that testing them on the foam roller and comparing 'good' side to complaint side is the quickest and easiest way. If the ITB is flared up, the complaint side will be significantly more tender than the 'good' side.

The Fix

HAM exercise from Chapter 1: Screening for Basic Structural Components and Chapter 3: Symmetry.

Using a foam roller will be very uncomfortable when the ITB is flared up (Fig. 49a and 49b). You will know that things are 'fixed' when it no longer feels terrible. I like to roll both legs to get a true picture of tightness.

Fig. 49a: Foam roller exercise, starting position

Fig. 49b: Foam roller exercise, final position

Band Walk

(see Chapter 3: Symmetry for images)

When the Gluteus Medius gets stronger, it will be able to provide enough hip control by itself and the ITB can return to being a secondary stabilizer.

2. Piriformis

This is a classic pain-in-the-butt injury. Most often it hurts when sitting due to pressure on the piriformis, which can make driving home from a long run an agonizing experience. Sometimes it will only flare up during long runs when it gets overworked.

The Fix:

I have found the pigeon stretch to be the best way to isolate and stretch this muscle (Fig. 50).

Fig. 50: Phases 1-5 of the Pigeon Stretch.

Band Walk

(see Chapter 3: Symmetry for images)

As with ITB problems, the piriformis is overused and inflamed when the glutes are not working properly due to either weakness or poor technique.

3. Chondromalacia Patella

This is probably the most common injury for runners, and mostly beginning runners. It is usually caused by the kneecap (patella) moving incorrectly in the groove in the knee. Over the years I have found that it takes a multi-prong approach to truly fix this problem.

The Fix:

A. Building up the vastus medialis oblique (VMO) muscle using chair squats with a ball (Fig. 51a and b).

1. Start: sit with good posture at edge of chair, squeeze standard ball (soccer/ volley / basketball) between knees and have feet slightly closer together than gap between knees. You should feel bow-legged.

2. Stand: while squeezing ball come to stand position with good posture. You will definitely be bowlegged.

3. Return to Sit and Repeat per program

Fig. 51a: Start position, sitting on edge of chair, bow-legged, squeezing a ball between the knees;
Fig. 51b: Middle position, standing while squeezing the ball with feet closer together than the knees.

B. Straight Leg Raise (SLR) (Fig. 52a and b).

Fig. 52a: SLR exercise (steps 1 and 2): 1. Lay on mat with one leg in bent knee position and the active leg flat; 2. Tighten the muscles of the Quads (top of Thigh) and slowly lift leg about 8 inches.

Fig. 52b: SLR exercise (steps 3 and 4): 3. Maintain the tight muscles and slowly lower the leg to the start position; 4. Repeat as many times as possible with good technique. If you are unable to keep the knee locked/ tight then stop the exercise as you could cause stress to knee cap.

C. Foam Roller for the Tight ITB

(see the section on ITB above)

We learned to include this after many clients did not respond to the basic program of VMO strengthening. Our 'AHA' moment was to realize that a tight or over-worked ITB would affect the line-of-pull of the patella. When we fixed this aspect, it was so much easier for the VMO to do its job.

D. Band Walking

(see Symmetry section)

4. PLANTAR FASCITIS

This is another very common ailment for runners. You can spend days looking at all the websites with numerous suggestions for treatment, many theories for why it occurs, etc. I will stay out of the discussion as that is not the focus of this book. However, I will say that a few common remedies that do work are:

A. Massage bottom of foot (where all the plantar fascia is located) with a tennis ball or golf ball (Fig. 53a and 53b). It will be one of those things that 'hurt so good'.

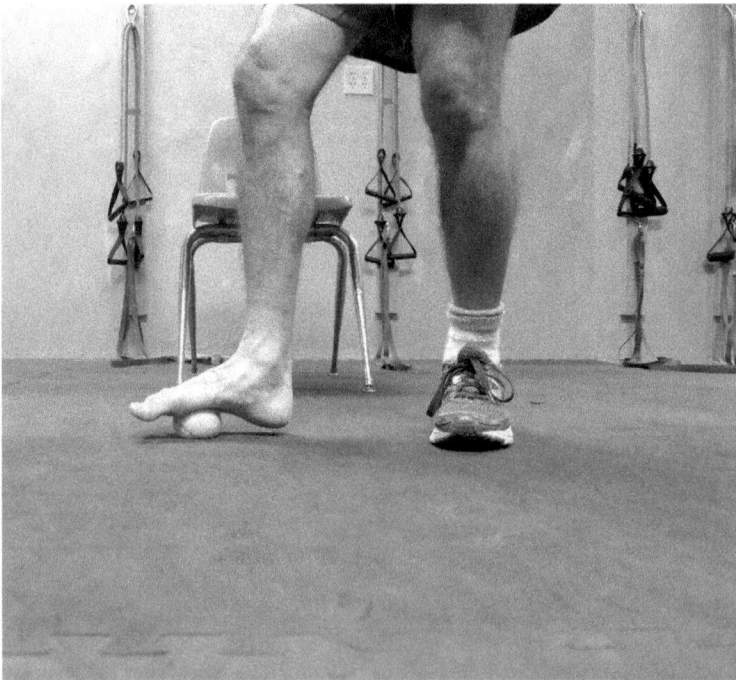

Fig. 53a: Starting position of foot massage

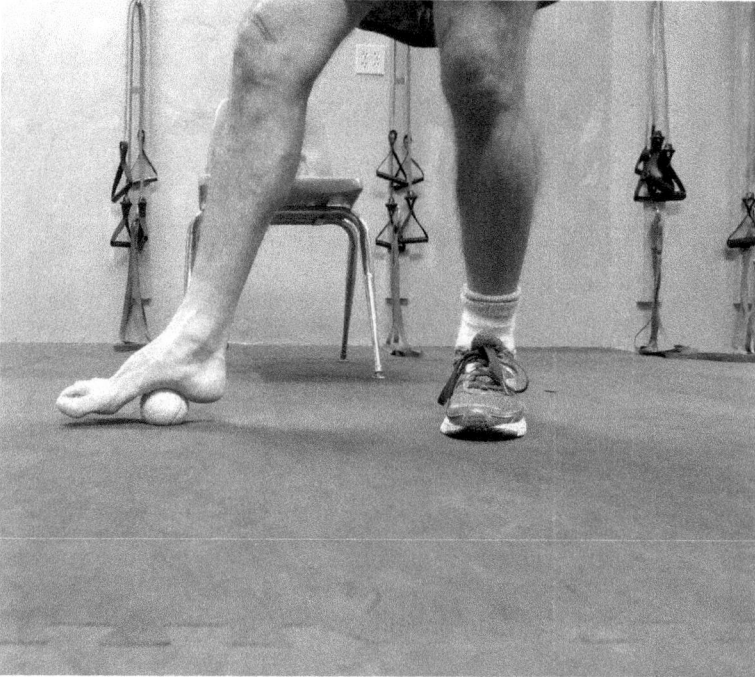

Fig. 53b: Ending position of foot massage.

B. Build up the muscles that support the arch of the foot and thereby reduce the stress on the fascia. This is the true long-term solution that does not rely on inserts or expensive orthotics (Fig. 54a and 54b). This is very simple and boring, which is why most people don't do it. Tsk Tsk.

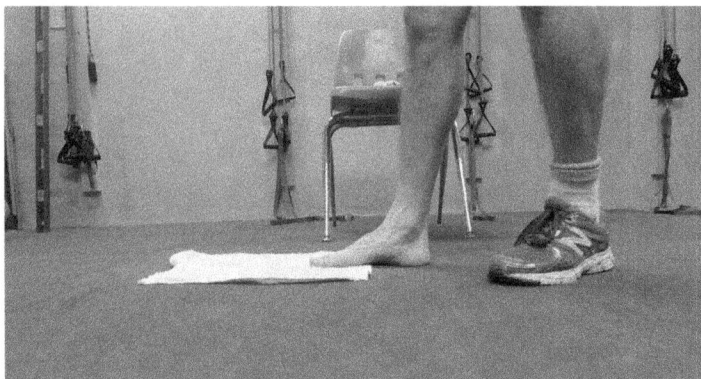

Fig. 54a: Starting position for foot arch exercise

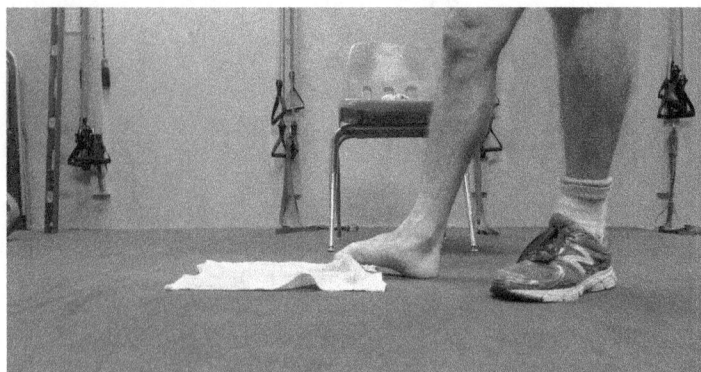

Fig. 54b: Ending position for foot arch exercise

Bibliography

Acetta, Randy and Wenneborg, Greg. *BASIC Training for Running*. (Tucson: Desert Southwest Fitness, 2003)

Acetta, Randy and Wenneborg, Greg. *Marathon Training*. (Tucson: Desert Southwest Fitness, 2003)

Burfoot, Amby. *Runner's World Complete Book of Running: Everything You Need to Run for Weight Loss, Fitness, and Competition*. (Emmaus, PA: Rodale Press, 1997)

Doherty, Ken. *Track & Field Omni Book*, 5th edition. (Mountain View, CA: TAFNEWS Press, 2007)

Fordyce, Bruce. *Marathon Runner's Handbook*. (Human Kinetics, 2002)

Futterman, Matthew. *Gait Analysis: The Serious Runner's Salvation*. (The Wall Street Journal, Sept. 22, 2014)

Livingstone, Keith. *Healthy Intelligent Training: The Proven Principles of Arthur Lydiard*. (Meyer & Meyer, 2010)

Noakes, Tim. *The Lore of Running*, 3rd Edition. (Leisure Press, 1991)

Running Times Magazine (Emmaus, PA: Rodale Inc.)

Runner's World Magazine (Emmaus, PA: Rodale Inc.)

Skidmore, Brook. "Olympic Style Lifting for Distance Runners" in *NSCA Performance Training Journal*, Vol 11, Issue 2

Tucker, Ross. *Runner's World The Runner's Body: How the Latest Exercise Science Can Help You Run Stronger, Longer, and Faster*. (Rodale Books, 2009)

Trail Runner Magazines (Carbondale, CO: Big Stone Pub.)

Yessis, Michael. *Explosive Running: Using the Science of Kinesiology to Improve your Performance*. (Chicago: Contemporary Books, 2000)

Glossary of Terms

Chondromalacia Patella: Chondromalacia patellae (also known as CMP) is a term that goes back eighty years. It originally meant "soft cartilage under the knee cap", a presumed cause of **pain** at the front and especially inner side of the knee. This condition often affects young, otherwise healthy individuals.

Chondromalacia is due to an irritation of the undersurface of the knee cap. The undersurface of the knee cap, or *patella*, is covered with a layer of smooth cartilage. This cartilage normally glides effortlessly across the knee during bending of the joint. However, in some individuals, the knee cap tends to rub against one side of the knee joint, and the cartilage surface becomes irritated, and knee pain is the result. (Source: WIKIPEDIA)

Inversion/Eversion: movement of the foot at the ankle joint. Inversion = turning the inside edge of foot (big toe side) upwards. Eversion = turning the outside edge (little toe side) of the foot upwards.

Medial Meniscus: The medial **meniscus** is a **fibrocartilage** semicircular band that spans the **knee** joint medially, located between the **medial condyle** of the **femur** and the **medial condyle** of the **tibia**. It is also referred to as the internal semilunar fibrocartilage. It is a common site of injury, especially if the knee is twisted. (Source: WIKIPEDIA)

Patellar Femoral Pain Sydrome: The cause of pain and dysfunction often results from either abnormal forces (e.g. increased pull of the lateral **quadricep** retinaculum with acute or chronic lateral PF subluxation/dislocation) or prolonged repetitive compressive or shearing forces (running or jumping) on the PF joint. The result is thinning and softening (**chondromalacia**) of the articular cartilage under the patella and/or on the medial or lateral femoral condyles, synovial irritation and inflammation and subchondral bony changes in the distal femur or patella known as "bone bruises". Secondary causes of PF Syndrome are fractures, internal knee derangement, osteoarthritis of the knee and bony tumors in or around the knee.

Specific populations at high risk of primary Patellofemoral Syndrome include runners, basketball players, young athletes and females especially those who have an increased angle of **genu valgus** (aka "Q-Angle" or commonly referred to as "knock-knees"). Typically patients will complain of localized anterior knee pain which is exacerbated by sports, walking, sitting for a long time, or stair climbing. Descending stairs may be worse than ascending. Unless there is an underlying pathology in the knee, swelling is usually mild to nil. Palpation, as well, is usually unremarkable. (Source: WIKIPEDIA)

Sacrum: commonly referred to as "your tailbone". The part of your pelvis in back at the base of your spine.

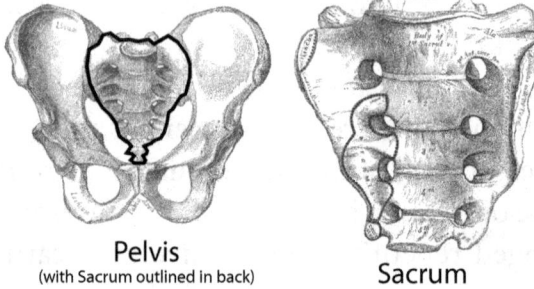

Pelvis
(with Sacrum outlined in back)

Sacrum

(Source: WIKIMEDIA COMMONS)

Stored Kinetic Energy: energy that is created when the impact of ground force reaction is converted into tensile energy in the calf muscle during landing.

Turf Toe: common condition in runners and athletes when their toes jam into the front of their shoes. This can create bruising of toes and blackened toenail from blood ulcers if severe.

Proprioception: ability to know where one's limb is in space; e.g. is my arm up in air or down by my side?

Plantar Flexion: action of pointing the foot downwards from neutral position.

Walking Lunge: act of slowly repeating the common exercise of lunging with alternating legs while appearing to be walking.